Government
Against Poverty

STUDIES IN SOCIAL ECONOMICS

TITLES PUBLISHED

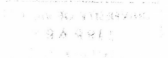

STUDIES IN SOCIAL ECONOMICS

Government Against Poverty

Joseph A. Kershaw

WITH THE ASSISTANCE OF

Paul N. Courant

THE BROOKINGS INSTITUTION
Washington, D.C.

ISBN 0–8157–4902–3
Library of Congress Catalog Card Number 78–111885

THE BROOKINGS INSTITUTION is an independent organization devoted to nonpartisan research, education, and publication in economics, government, foreign policy, and the social sciences generally. Its principal purposes are to aid in the development of sound public policies and to promote public understanding of issues of national importance.

The Institution was founded on December 8, 1927, to merge the activities of the Institute for Government Research, founded in 1916, the Institute of Economics, founded in 1922, and the Robert Brookings Graduate School of Economics and Government, founded in 1924.

The general administration of the Institution is the responsibility of a self-perpetuating Board of Trustees. The trustees are likewise charged with maintaining the independence of the staff and fostering the most favorable conditions for creative research and education. The immediate direction of the policies, program, and staff of the Institution is vested in the President, assisted by an advisory council chosen from the staff of the Institution.

In publishing a study, the Institution presents it as a competent treatment of a subject worthy of public consideration. The interpretations and conclusions in such publications are those of the author or authors and do not purport to represent the views of the other staff members, officers, or trustees of the Brookings Institution.

Foreword

In a period of great affluence, some 25 million Americans—more than 12 percent of the total population—were living in poverty in 1968. This was four years after passage of the Economic Opportunity Act of 1964 declaring that United States policy was "to eliminate the paradox of poverty in the midst of plenty" by opening to all the opportunity for education and training, for work, and for living "in decency and dignity." To accomplish these ends the Congress created an Office of Economic Opportunity, with a director who was not only to manage the new programs of the OEO but also "to assist the President in coordinating the antipoverty efforts of all Federal agencies."

This volume is an account of government efforts on behalf of the poor since the declaration of "unconditional war on poverty" —efforts made not only through the Office of Economic Opportunity, but also through significant broadening of social security, aid to education, public assistance in housing, and in other ways. With the special knowledge he acquired as assistant director of OEO in 1965 and 1966, Joseph A. Kershaw, now with the division of education and research of the Ford Foundation, describes the successes and failures of the antipoverty campaign and contemplates its future.

The author wishes to thank Paul N. Courant, a former Brookings staff member now serving on the staff of the Council of Economic Advisers, for his valuable contributions to the project and his refinements of the manuscript. He is also grateful to Malcolm Goetz, a Yale Law School student, who assisted in many ways during the preparation of the first draft and was especially helpful in

vii

straightening out details of the chapter on income maintenance. Throughout the project Joseph A. Pechman, director of economic studies at Brookings, was a steady source of encouragement and support. The constructive suggestions of three anonymous critics selected by Brookings also improved the manuscript greatly. Evelyn P. Fisher, assisted by Margaret Lyerly, carefully checked the statistical material for consistency and accuracy; the manuscript was edited by Frances M. Shattuck, and the index was prepared by Helen B. Eisenhart.

This volume is the seventh of the Brookings Studies in Social Economics, a special program of research and education on selected topics in the fields of health, education, social security, and welfare.

The views expressed here are those of the author and should not be attributed to the Office of Economic Opportunity, the Ford Foundation, or the trustees, officers, or staff members of the Brookings Institution.

KERMIT GORDON
President

April 1970
Washington, D.C.

Contents

CHAPTER I

Introduction

America is a land of untold wealth. The United States is currently producing goods and services at an annual value of close to a trillion dollars. This output is a substantial multiple of that of the nearest competitor, whether on a gross or per capita basis, and there is an order of magnitude between the United States and the underdeveloped world.

Why, then, so much talk of poverty? The answer is that, in all this affluence, there are substantial numbers of Americans who, by almost any definition, are living in poverty, sometimes abject poverty. Some Americans do not participate in the general affluence; some will not do so even when continued growth further increases this wealth, unless public policy is changed and succeeds in altering some of the fundamental relationships in society.

Poverty is nothing new, in this or in any other country. What is new is a nation's explicit recognition that poverty is a social evil, and that something should and can be done about speeding up its elimination. Perhaps there is a growing assurance that the country's affluence makes it practical to think seriously of such a goal. It may be, too, that the nation's conscience has been troubled by the disconcerting contrasts between the growing comforts enjoyed by most and the miseries of the urban and rural slums experienced by some.

Whatever the immediate reason, a war on poverty in the United States has been declared. In the Economic Opportunity Act of 1964 the Congress solemnly stated it to be "the policy of the

1

United States to eliminate the paradox of poverty in the midst of plenty in this Nation . . ." Note that the operative verb in this declaration is to eliminate, not to ameliorate—the intention is somehow to put an end to the condition. This is what is new. Nations the world over, including the United States, have long been concerned with making the lot of the poor more bearable, but here for the first time it has been resolved to root out poverty altogether. It is a novel resolution.

This volume is an attempt to describe and assess the first few years of the effort, to see what was done and why, and to sort out those things done well and those done badly. The outcome has been disappointing on balance, though some highly beneficial results have no doubt been achieved. The extent of poverty has continued to decline as economic growth persisted, but it is difficult to attribute much of this to the war on poverty, as of early 1970. In large part the modesty of the achievement is accounted for by the nation's unwillingness (some would say inability, but they are wrong) to devote the quantity of resources visualized in 1964 as necessary over the coming years. The war on poverty has been a major casualty of the war in Southeast Asia. In spite of the fact that expenditures on the poor have risen substantially since 1964, these increases have not enabled the government programs to reach more than a fraction of those in need.

The war on poverty is frequently thought of as those programs administered by the Office of Economic Opportunity. These have perhaps made the most noise, in that they have been politically most controversial. They have also been directed at curing rather than simply ameliorating poverty. But OEO programs have never commanded more than a small fraction of the federal government's poverty dollar, nor of the amounts spent by state and local governments on the low-income population. The concern here is with the broader war, not just with the Office of Economic Opportunity. But since most of what is novel in the war on poverty has been either directed or funded by OEO (the major exceptions are Medicare and expenditures under the Elementary and Secondary Education Act of 1965), a perhaps disproportionate share of attention will be aimed toward that agency and its progress and problems.

Chapter 2 attempts to arrive at a plausible definition of poverty in the United States in the 1960s, with full recognition that there are no absolutes that are applicable. The federal government has adopted a definition, based largely on income and family size; it is far from perfect but has at least a rationale, and it seems to work. Using this definition, the chapter examines the characteristics of the American poor—sex, race, family composition, relation to the labor force, location, and the like.

Chapters 3 and 4 first study the legislation adopted in 1964 and amendments of later years, then the government's diagnosis and the nature of the proposed cure. The Economic Opportunity Act was designed to attack the problems of people and environments, both of which were regarded as deficient. The idea was to create conditions that would enable people to help themselves—better education, health, housing, jobs, all to be achieved through community action and initiative with help from the federal treasury. These chapters also discuss the innovations brought by the Elementary and Secondary Education Act of 1965, particularly Title I, and recent amendments to the Social Security Act.

Since unemployment, underemployment, and failure to participate in the labor force are so central to the low-income problem, Chapter 5 is devoted to the general problems of manpower. Some of these problems are macroeconomic, such as the appropriate fiscal and monetary policies to assure a high level of employment. Some are training problems, a complex area which has at times involved OEO (for example, the Job Corps), the Department of Labor (for example, the Manpower Administration), and the Department of Health, Education, and Welfare (for example, vocational education and rehabilitation). Some problems seem to be largely those of welfare, aimed at the uneducated and chronically unemployed; these are most difficult and unyielding. Manpower policies for many years were concerned with increasing skills and finding jobs for those who were unemployed but quite employable. As concern for the truly hard core has increased, it has become apparent that entirely new approaches are called for, but these have not been easy to come by. Although many answers are still proving to be elusive, it is clear that the last few years have at least brought increased knowledge about the nature of hard-core unemployment.

During the months or years while attempts are made to improve skills, attitudes, and other qualities that may be deficient, what happens to the poor? The potentially trainable people as well as those who cannot be expected to solve their problems through the labor market (husbandless mothers, most of the aged, the handicapped) need financial support. For the last generation state welfare systems, with federal financing, have supposedly performed this function. As an income maintenance system for the poor, however, welfare has been coming under attack by more and more thoughtful observers and participants. Chapter 6 surveys the system and attempts to understand its shortcomings and achievements, concluding that it leaves a great deal to be desired and needs either wholesale changes or, preferably, entirely new ideas. Two of these new ideas—a system of children's allowances and the negative income tax—are examined, with the latter being preferred.

Finally (except for an overall assessment), there is a discussion of three fairly technical problems. One is the way in which a comprehensive plan for five years is drawn up, how the costs of alternative goals are calculated. This is a relatively new technique in government, though the military establishment has been doing it for some time. The second concerns the whole problem of comprehensive evaluation. How is a decision arrived at that a dollar spent one way is better than a dollar spent another way? Evaluation and planning are closely related, since a plan will be efficient only if it contains the "best" combination of expenditures. The poverty officials have pioneered in some significant ways with these problems, with possible substantial consequences for better government planning and administration in the future. The third problem—program management—was complex because of the director's assignment to coordinate all antipoverty efforts. Some were programs operated by OEO; some were delegated by him to other agencies; still others were completely outside his agency. Under these circumstances coordination was exceedingly difficult.

CHAPTER II

Who Are the Poor?

Specifying the boundaries of poverty, both in the past and in the present, is important since it will determine the quantity of resources required to solve the problem. The question becomes critical when the chance of reaching a solution within a reasonable time period is explored.

The word "poverty" has no absolute meaning, and there is no generally satisfactory definition that people can agree on and work with. This is unfortunate since it is important to distinguish the poor from the nonpoor. A definition of some sort has to be used and, once adopted, it must determine that some families and individuals are officially "poor" and hence eligible for benefits and that others are not.

Most attempts to define poverty have been mainly concerned with some "necessary" amount of income—necessary, that is, to command some minimum quantity of goods and services. This concern was implicit in Franklin D. Roosevelt's phrase in his second inaugural address of January 1937: "I see one-third of a nation ill-housed, ill-clad, ill-nourished." It is explicit in the definition now used in the United States war on poverty. The problem is to characterize or describe this minimum quantity of goods and services. No two observers come up with the same quantity, and any quantity selected changes over time.

One of the first attempts to define a "poverty line" was made by Robert Hunter in 1904. He estimated that a family of average size —father, mother, and three children—would need $460 per year to meet essential expenses ($300 in the South).[1] The price level has more than quadrupled since then; this would, therefore, amount to more than $2,100 in today's prices, whereas the 1968 definition sets the line at $4,191 for such a family.

Between 1904 and 1965 other attempts at establishing a poverty line were made. In 1949, for example, a report on low-income families by the Joint Committee on the Economic Report concentrated on a boundary line of $2,000 for a city family of two or more.[2] The line has continued to rise over time and no doubt will do so in the future as well. This is partly because the style of life changes and luxuries become necessities—a car is frequently required to get to work, a radio is seen as essential, and so on. As incomes rise the notions of necessities and luxuries are revised, for those better off as well as for the less fortunate. Most people regard electricity and inside plumbing as necessities today, whereas once they were considered frills. In short, any income definition adopted should not be regarded as immutable.

In January 1964 President Lyndon B. Johnson in his State of the Union message first called public attention to the need for a war on poverty. The basic features of the attack were outlined later that month in the report of the Council of Economic Advisers. At that time the council defined as poor any individual with an income below $1,500 annually, and any family with less than $3,000 (in 1962 prices). These figures were rounded and generalized from the results of a study made by the Social Security Administration, and were used by the council only to indicate the size of the poverty problem. The council pointed out that "no measure of poverty as simple as the one used here, would be suitable for determining eligibility for particular benefits or participation in particular programs."[3]

---

[1] *Poverty* (Macmillan, 1904), p. 52.

[2] However, the committee noted that the figure was not intended to be a definition of low income. *Low-Income Families and Economic Stability*, Materials on the Problem of Low-Income Families Assembled by the Staff of the Subcommittee on Low-Income Families, 81 Cong. 1 sess. (1949), p. 2.

[3] *Economic Report of the President, January 1964*, Chap. 2. The quotation appears on p. 58.

OEO Definition

Something over a year later, the newly created Office of Economic Opportunity modified the definition in several respects, though it continued to be based on the social security study. Such a definition had to be framed to serve three distinct purposes. First, it had to distinguish the poor from the nonpoor so that the poor could be counted. In other words, a statistical record had to be maintained to indicate how the war on poverty was going. For this purpose it did not matter greatly where the line was drawn since it was changes over time that mattered.

Second, the definition had to be simple enough to be operational—poor people were eligible for benefits, the nonpoor normally were not. Those administering the various programs had to be able to recognize the poor. For this purpose it mattered a great deal indeed where the line was drawn, and from time to time there has been pressure to raise it (to increase the number eligible for benefits). Such pressures, for example, existed in connection with both Head Start and Neighborhood Youth Corps, particularly in the early months of the programs.

Third, for many programs funds had to be geographically distributed in an equitable fashion, according to the statute, and the location of the poor was a part of the determination of what was equitable. Rural-nonrural distinctions, as an example, became most significant in this sense. One explanation of the troubles the definition brought to the agency lies in the difficulties inherent in an attempt to develop one that would serve all three purposes.

The official OEO definition, like the earlier one of the council, started from an "economy" food plan for "temporary or emergency use when funds are low." The plan, developed by the Department of Agriculture, began with the cost of the amount of food needed to supply nutritional adequacy for an individual. The economy budget required more expenditures for men and teen-age boys, whose needs are greater, than for women and young children. The Social Security Administration developed age-sex prototypes for each family size based on 1960 census data; this in effect created an average family of each size. The economy food plan for the age and sex of each individual in the typical family was summed up to give an economy plan for each family size. "In January 1964, this plan suggested foods costing $4.60 a week per person, an average of only 22 cents a meal per person in a 4-person family."[4]

Food expenditures were then assumed to absorb one-third of total income for families of four people, a proportion found to be typical of spending patterns for people in the lowest income range, as shown in studies by the Department of Agriculture and Bureau of Labor Statistics. Smaller families were believed to have larger fixed costs per person; for example, rent might increase as a family increased from two to three members, but was unlikely to increase by 50 percent; therefore food expenditure was assumed to be 27 percent of a typical couple's income. Unrelated individuals were assumed to require 80 percent of the income of couples, for the same reason. These calculations gave poverty line annual incomes for 1964 of $1,540 for one person, $3,130 for four, and $5,090 for seven or more.[5]

Interestingly enough, varying the income line for family size did not make any appreciable change in the total number estimated to be in poverty from the much simpler council definition. It did, however, change the composition significantly in two ways: It increased the number of poor children by four million because the line rose as size of family increased, and it decreased the number of aged poor because so many of the aged were in families of two, with a correspondingly lower poverty line.[6]

Another modification of the council's simple definition had to do with the treatment of the farm poor. Originally the social security study had indicated that income in kind (mostly housing and home-grown food) enjoyed by farmers ought to reduce the poverty line for farm families by 40 percent. Further research, particularly in the Department of Agriculture, indicated that 40 percent was too severe a reduction—in particular, home-grown food appeared to be much less important to farmers than it once was. The

[4] Mollie Orshansky, "Counting the Poor: Another Look at the Poverty Profile," *Social Security Bulletin,* Vol. 28 (January 1965), p. 6.

[5] For a thorough explanation of how the lines were drawn, see *ibid.,* pp. 3-10.

[6] *Economic Report of the President, January 1965,* p. 163.

discount was changed, therefore, from 40 to 30 percent, and the official tables showed farm family poverty lines at 70 percent of those of nonfarm families. Although this change increased the number of farm residents who were officially poor, the number remained significantly less than it was under the simpler council definition (4.0 million rather than 4.9 million). The discount was changed again in 1969 from 30 to 15 percent, further increasing the number of farm poor.[7] Whether this level of discount is rational will be considered later.

After the adoption of this modified definition, still another change was made. Lumping together all families of seven or more proved to be unworkable. It first became apparent in 1965 when many applicants for the Neighborhood Youth Corps from families with eight or nine or ten children were being turned away because the family income exceeded $5,090. The maximum family size of seven (typically five children and the parents) had been imposed because it was assumed that there was no need to make provision for families above that size. This assumption was found to be unwarranted, and the definition was extended by OEO to encompass families of up to thirteen. The line for such a family was set at $7,635, an increase of $500 for each additional child.[8] The agency resolved not to go beyond that figure on the ground that economies of scale could be expected to offset any additional members beyond thirteen!

Table 1 indicates the poverty lines for 1966 and 1968, by size of family, for farm and nonfarm families. The figures for 1966 were generalized and averaged and rounded from the many families studied by the Social Security Administration. Beyond six, simple $500 increments were used for nonfarm families and $350 (70 percent of $500) for those on farms. The figures for 1968 are based on the revised definition of the Bureau of the Census.

The poverty lines are adjusted each year to reflect price changes. Until 1969 the revisions were based on the average per capita cost

[7] Orshansky, "Counting the Poor," p. 11, and "Who's Who Among the Poor: A Demographic View of Poverty," *Social Security Bulletin,* Vol. 28 (July 1965), pp. 9, 10; U.S. Bureau of the Census, *Current Population Reports,* Series P-23, No. 28, "Revision in Poverty Statistics, 1959 to 1968" (1969), p. 1.

[8] U.S. Office of Economic Opportunity, "Dimensions of Poverty in 1964–1965–1966" (Dec. 10, 1968; processed).

TABLE I

Average Thresholds of Poverty, 1966 and 1968

| Family size (persons) | Annual cash income (in dollars) | | | |
| | 1966 | | 1968[a] | |
	Nonfarm	Farm	Nonfarm	Farm
1	1,635	1,145	1,748	1,487
2	2,115	1,475	2,262	1,904
3	2,600	1,815	2,774	2,352
4	3,335	2,345	3,553	3,034
5	3,930	2,755	4,188	3,577
6	4,410	3,090	4,706	4,021
7	4,910	3,440	5,789	4,916
8	5,410	3,790		
9	5,910	4,140		
10	6,410	4,490		
11	6,910	4,840		
12	7,410	5,190		
13 or more	7,910	5,540		

Sources: 1966 figures from U.S. Office of Economic Opportunity, "Dimensions of Poverty in 1964–1965–1966" (Dec. 10, 1968; processed), Table 1; 1968 figures from revised definition of poverty adopted as the official standard in 1969, U.S. Bureau of the Census, *Current Population Reports*, Series P-60, No. 68, "Poverty in the United States: 1959 to 1968" (1969), p. 11.

a. Figures for seven persons are also for more than seven.

of items in the economy food budget. During the 1960s, increases in the cost of the goods in the economy food budget did not keep pace with increases in the overall cost of living. Consequently, the consumer price index was adopted as the basis for the annual adjustments.[9] Unless otherwise indicated, the data on the poverty population shown in this volume are based on the revised definition, which includes the 15 percent discount for farm poor discussed above. In general, the revisions, which have been applied to all data for years from 1959 on, have caused only relatively minor changes in the size and composition of the population designated as poor.

Deficiencies of Official Definition

The poverty definition falls short in a number of respects. First, there is no sanctity about the food budget on which it is based. In-

[9] U.S. Bureau of the Census, "Revision in Poverty Statistics, 1959 to 1968."

deed, the Department of Agriculture developed two budgets: the economy budget, used in the official definition, and a low-cost budget, which is about one-third higher. Between these two the choice can only be arbitrary. There may, in fact, be strong reason for preferring the low-cost budget, since the economy budget is specifically characterized as one on which people could be expected to feed themselves temporarily, during an emergency. Is it appropriate to use such a standard as a long-run measure of poverty? Similarly, one might also question the assumption that poor families spend one-third of their incomes on food. To these and other queries there are no scientific right answers; the only question is whether the consequences look plausible and reasonable.

Perhaps more basically, the definition leaves assets out of account entirely. The real concern should be with expenditures rather than income; the poverty definition takes income as a proxy for expenditures. There are bound to be some cases, therefore, where fairly well-to-do persons are classed in the poverty category. No attempt has been made to incorporate the possession of assets into the definition, both because of the administrative problems that would be created and because of the presumption that the poor have few assets. The Council of Economic Advisers has stated that "average (median) net asset holdings of poor families amounted to only $2,760 at the end of 1962. The bulk of these assets consisted of equity in a home and thus could not be easily converted into consumption,"[10] although they would normally contribute to housing costs in a minor way as imputed rents. Consequently, although there may be some anomalies created by this failure to take assets into account, no doubt their total magnitude is slight.

Another problem is inherent in the farm-nonfarm distinction. That farmers can do as well as nonfarmers, with somewhat less cash income, seems obvious, but the case for 70 percent or 85 percent (as against 60 or 80) is not easy to make. Furthermore, careful analysis of the problem suggests that a rural-nonrural distinction would make more sense than that of farm-nonfarm. It is living out of the city that makes housing cheaper; it is the availability

[10] *Economic Report of the President, January 1965*, p. 163.

of space that makes home-grown food possible. But to change the definition to account for this would make suddenly ineligible for poverty benefits many rural "poor" who have been part of the programs. Secretary of Agriculture Orville Freeman argued persistently that the definition was unfair in calling many of his clients nonpoor. Needless to say, he would not have regarded the extension of the 70 percent rule to rural nonfarmers as a solution; he would have liked the discount eliminated for farmers.

A more serious deficiency is the failure of the definition to distinguish among different regions of the country. One's intuition, if nothing else, argues that a family of four at a given income is poorer in Harlem than one in Tupelo, Mississippi. Cost of living differences, even if available, would not be adequate for correction of this disparity. Also important are such things as climate, accepted style of life, and transportation facilities and requirements. On the other hand, there are many free public services which are much more available in cities.

An interesting attempt to come to grips with this problem was made early in the poverty agency's history. The assumption was made that families in different areas were equally poor when they spent equal proportions of their incomes on food. Then the level of money incomes at which this proportion was equal was examined for four areas of the United States: North East, North Central, South, and West.[11] The results seemed intuitively reasonable for urban, rural, and nonfarm in each of the four regions.

But this does not solve the problem. These regions are still enormous, and it would probably be necessary to separate a dozen or two of the largest cities and call them additional areas. Furthermore, it was found that the two regions departing farthest from the norm (the North East and the South) were contiguous. It would have created administrative chaos to have the poverty line at $3,600 or $2,800, depending on which side of the street or state border or Mason-Dixon line a family lived. Thus this idea too was dropped; the general and uniform level, with all its faults, seemed less cumbersome than the refinement.

[11] Harold W. Watts, "The Iso-Prop Index: An Approach to the Determination of Differential Poverty Income Thresholds," *Journal of Human Resources,* Vol. 2 (Winter 1967), pp. 3–18.

The basic problem here is clear enough. To operate programs, simplicity and rough justice are essential. To be completely fair and rational, on the other hand, every family situation needs to be taken into account separately. What is required in a definition is the proper combination of reasonableness and simplicity, but under any combination selected it will always be possible to point out individual cases where the application of the definition appears either not simple or not reasonable.

One final defect deserves brief mention. The official definition, like any based on income, assumes that money will be spent wisely. The $4.60 per person per week for food had to buy the right kinds of food at the best prices obtainable. The total budget of $13.80 per week per person had to be spent carefully; it could not go for liquor or dope, nor for expensive used cars, nor for goods bought on credit at exorbitant rates. But the poor are rarely good buyers. Frequently they buy in quantities that are too small, and they have little ability to sense a bargain. When the poor are also Negro, the constraints that keep them in the ghetto frequently force them to buy where prices are high and credit even more so, and to pay rents that are pushed up by artificial constraints on the supply of housing.[12]

What can be said of the official definition in view of all of these obvious deficiencies? One point stands out: it works. Although the definition undoubtedly classifies some poor people as nonpoor, it classifies very few nonpoor as poor. Objections are raised from time to time, but rarely does anyone assert that it is enabling nonpoor to receive benefits or claim that any appreciable number of those counted as poor are really nonpoor. The reason would seem to be that the definition is a severe one. It is perhaps too severe in that many in need are ineligible for aid, but though some funds may go to people less poor than others because of the vagaries of the definition, they do not go to nonpoor instead of poor. This is very significant where resources are severely limited, as they have been in the case of the war on poverty. This implies that there is some absolute, correct characterization of poor, though there really

[12] Alan Batchelder, "Poverty: The Special Case of the Negro," in Burton A. Weisbrod (ed.), *The Economics of Poverty: An American Paradox* (Prentice-Hall, 1965), pp. 100–04.

is not. But the argument is that the definition is severe enough to enable reasonable men to agree that, wherever that absolute, correct characterization, it lies within the official definition. No doubt there would be more controversy if the available funds made it possible to come near to saturating the population described as poor. In the absence of this, questions about who benefits are minimal.

Concepts of Poverty

If there is no significant pressure for downward change in the official operational definition, there is intellectual disagreement on the whole concept of how poverty should be described. One group argues that the significant question is the income difference between low-income groups and the rest.[13] An absolute standard is like a will-o'-the-wisp, and will change over time. What is needed, this group feels, is something that expresses the frustrations inevitable when people see that almost everybody else has more income, regardless of the absolute level. A frequent suggestion to put this into operational terms is to define as poor all those whose income is less than half the median income level.

Until this notion is pushed to extremes it has considerable merit. Indeed, one would probably find that as ideas of the proper income to determine poverty have changed over time (always upward), they are not far from half the median. So one could argue that in the ranges regarded as relevant, such a definition would not be far from what is being used. At very low or very high income it seems to make little sense. If some have only one yacht, two homes, and three automobiles, while others have a multiple of these, poverty has lost its meaning. Also, if some sort of socialism or communism resulted in drastically lower total incomes but somehow divided them equally, it would hardly make sense to say that poverty had been eliminated.

[13] Victor R. Fuchs has written persuasively in this vein. See his "Toward a Theory of Poverty," in Task Force on Economic Growth and Opportunity, *The Concept of Poverty* (Chamber of Commerce of the United States, 1965), pp. 69–91. See also his "Redefining Poverty and Redistributing Income," *The Public Interest* (Summer 1967), pp. 88–95.

This line of argument, however, does focus on the very important matter of the distribution of income, and that is healthy, and bears directly on considerations of poverty. It is significant that the share of the lowest fifth of our income receivers has not been rising. "The lowest one-fifth of the consumer units (families and unattached individuals) got 4.1 per cent of the total family personal income in 1935, 5.0 per cent in 1947, and 4.6 per cent in 1962."[14] At the very least, and at low levels of absolute income, the failure of poor families to improve their relative situations over time is frustrating and must bear on the quality of poverty.

The use of a definition based on median income would make explicit the desirability of altering the distribution of income in favor of the poor, and perhaps this would be a good thing. But most measures taken to raise the level of incomes of the poor in fact do tend to bring about the desired change in income distribution. In the short run, where median income is not changing rapidly, the difference between this definition and the official one seems small, certainly in operational terms.

Finally, a considerable and eloquent school of thought argues that nonincome factors are the significant ones. Perhaps Oscar Lewis, who originated the term "culture of poverty," and Michael Harrington, whose *The Other America* was so instrumental in awakening Americans to the evils of poverty, are the leading voices here,[15] though there are others. These observers characterize people as poor when they live in ghettos, feel antagonistic toward the police, lack political power, have inferior public services (especially education), are discriminated against (particularly on racial grounds), and are generally unable to participate in the so-called mainstream of American life.

Again there is much merit in such an alternative view of poverty. And the community action part of the war on poverty pays more than lip service to these ideas. Within the scheme of community action, "target areas" are defined as being low-income areas, but the entire population of such areas is treated as if it were in

[14] Robert J. Lampman, "Income Distribution and Poverty," in Margaret S. Gordon (ed.), *Poverty in America* (Chandler, 1965), p. 105.

[15] Lewis, *Five Families: Mexican Case Studies in the Culture of Poverty* (Basic Books, 1959); Harrington, *The Other America: Poverty in the United States* (Macmillan, 1962).

need of aid regardless of individual incomes, and is thus entitled and encouraged to participate in most of the community action program. It is frequently the case that a substantial portion of the population of the target area (sometimes over half) have incomes above the relevant poverty line. Thus there is implicit recognition of the idea that in such cases all people within the community are poor in the sense described above, not necessarily because of income, but because their background and environment are so unfavorable. Those who argue this position admit, to be sure, that there is a rough coincidence between low income and poverty as they define it. When the two diverge, they maintain, it is poverty in this social sense rather than income that should determine the direction of social and governmental concern.

But to use such a definition across the board in poverty programs would hardly be possible. Eligibility determinations are made daily in hundreds of cases, by people who are not professional sociologists. The income criterion is not easy in many cases, but it is far simpler than a set of nonquantifiable social characteristics with which most laymen are ill at ease. It must be recognized that income is a fairly good proxy for all of the objectives of the program, and that its use does get the resources generally to the right places, or at least not to the wrong places.[16]

The Poor Classified

There remains the task of sketching who the poor are, given the official definition. Although detailed information is always a year or two old, and the number of poor at any given recent period is no more than an estimate, since only a census could give accurate data, these estimates are adequate to afford a feel for the size of the problem and for its general nature.

There were in 1968 some 25 million Americans who were poor, according to the official definition.[17] In recent years this number has been declining by between one and two million a year in spite

[16] The distinction is important. Resources do not get to the rural poor (the right place) as much as they should, but not because they are going to the wrong place. They go to the urban poor, which is also a right place.

[17] U.S. Bureau of the Census, "Revision in Poverty Statistics, 1959 to 1968," p. 6.

TABLE 2

Number and Percentage of Poor Persons,
by Selected Characteristics, 1968[a]

(Numbers in thousands)

Age and family status	Total		With male head				With female head			
			White		Nonwhite[b]		White		Nonwhite[b]	
	Number	Percent	Number	Percent	Number	Percent	Number	Percent	Number	Percent
Unrelated[c]	4,694	34.0	1,000	23.3	320	34.8	2,849	37.1	525	56.7
Under 65	2,110	24.8	529	16.8	216	29.0	1,070	26.7	295	47.2
Age 65 and over	2,584	48.8	471	41.1	104	59.7	1,779	48.5	230	76.5
In families	20,695	11.3	9,995	6.7	3,710	22.9	3,551	29.1	3,439	58.7
Head	5,047	10.0	2,595	6.3	697	18.9	1,021	25.2	734	52.9
Children under 18	10,739	15.3	4,298	7.8	2,032	28.3	2,075	44.4	2,334	70.4
Other members	4,909	7.8	3,102	5.8	981	18.5	455	13.1	371	32.1
Total	25,389	12.8	10,995	7.1	4,030	23.6	6,400	32.3	3,964	58.4

Source: U.S. Bureau of the Census, *Current Population Reports*, Series P-60, No. 68, "Poverty in the United States: 1959 to 1968" (1969), pp. 21, 24, 34, 35, 37, 38.
a. Percentages are the poor as a percentage of the total population in each category.
b. Negro and other races.
c. Age 14 and over.

of a population increase of some two to three million annually. Every kind of American is represented, including those in families headed by a white, Anglo-Saxon male in the prime working age group and employed full time. But the incidence varies sharply among different kinds of people living under different circumstances.

In 1968, 12.8 percent of all Americans fell in the poverty group (see Table 2). Those groups with a poverty incidence substantially higher than average include aged unrelated individuals (49 percent), nonwhite families with male heads (23 percent), and nonwhite families with female heads (59 percent). The categories are not exclusive, and any person who is in more than one class has that much more chance to be poor. Living in the South enhances the chance, too, as does belonging to a large family.

Concentration of poverty exists in geographic areas as well, with extreme concentrations in some areas.[18] For example, in one civil

[18] The following data are based on unpublished tabulations of 1959 income distribution data for people in all the minor civil divisions of the country made for OEO by the U.S. Bureau of the Census. The data are based on the unrevised definition of poverty, since the tabulations were made before the revision.

division in Baltimore, there were 183 five-person families; their median family income was $2,522. Of the total, 147 were in the lowest decile of income for five-person families in Maryland; the median income for these 147 was $1,951. The comparable poverty line for five-person families was $3,605 in 1959. Of the members of these families, only 89 were males aged twenty-five to sixty-four. The people in five-person families dwelling in this area were 100 percent nonwhite. These figures show the level of concentration of poverty that is possible in urban areas.

The concentration possible in rural areas is demonstrated by income data for one county in the state of Mississippi. Of the 3,869 families in the county, 2,128 (or 55 percent) were poor by 1959 income figures; 105 had no income, and 872 had incomes from $1 to $999. Thus 25 percent of all families in the county had incomes below $1,000. Of the 977 families, 269 had five or more persons. As in the Baltimore area, nonwhites fell dramatically into the poverty category. Of the county's 1,560 nonwhite families, 1,357 (87 percent) were poor; 643 (41 percent) had incomes of less than $1,000; 1,003 (64 percent) had incomes of less than $2,000. None had an income of $10,000 or more, and only 119 (8 percent) had incomes of over $4,000. Nonwhites also had the larger families; 328 of the 361 families of eight or more persons were nonwhite, as were 815 of the 1,351 families of five or more.

This chapter has shown that there is much that is relevant to both the economic and social aspects of poverty in America which is not taken explicitly into account by the official definition, as illustrated by the poverty lines shown in Table 1. Yet implicit within the operation of the war on poverty and the official definition is a recognition of most of these considerations. Any program aimed at increasing the financial welfare of poor people will favorably affect income distribution. The problems of the culture of poverty and the social alienation of the poor are recognized in the definition of target areas, in which the local community action project seeks to improve both the incomes and the outlooks of the community, whether or not the individual is under the poverty line. That any operating definition of poverty must be easy to administer can hardly be disputed, and that the definition now used has resulted in benefits to the nonpoor has not been widely asserted.

Under the rather strict definition now in use there are approximately 25 million people the United States regards as poor. We turn now to a description and analysis of what the nation is trying to do about them.

CHAPTER III

The New Legislation

In a dynamic society like that of the United States, one of the most important characteristics is growth. Population grows every year but income grows, in almost every year, even faster, so that on the average people are richer in each succeeding year than they were in the last. One consequence is that by most measures the number and percentage of Americans whose incomes are below any stated figure decline each year. By the simple poverty definition of the Council of Economic Advisers—$3,000 income for families (corrected for price changes)—the number of poor families declined from 32 percent of the total in 1947 to 19 percent in 1963.[1] Over a longer period, from 1929 to 1960, the incidence of poverty fell by almost half, although the poverty line was allowed to rise gradually.[2]

Robert J. Lampman has pointed out that this process is by no means a straightforward one. Some groups exit rapidly from poverty as economic growth takes place; others seem affected not at all. Some demographic factors help the reduction in poverty: people are moving off farms, from low-income to high-income states, and to higher income occupations. Other demographic factors work in the opposite direction: families with no wage earner are increasing in relation to the total, as are nonwhites. These factors interact in complex ways and change the nature of the poverty population

[1] Herman P. Miller, "Changes in the Number and Composition of the Poor," in Margaret S. Gordon (ed.), *Poverty in America* (Chandler, 1965), p. 89.
[2] R. A. Gordon, "An Economist's View of Poverty," *ibid.*, p. 6.

over time. For one example, "the poorest state, Mississippi, had 70 per cent of its families in poverty in 1949, when the richest state, Connecticut, had 20 per cent in poverty. In 1959 the incidence rates were 52 for Mississippi and 9 for Connecticut."[3] Thus the improvement was spotty, and the suspicion grew that substantial numbers of the poor were unaffected by economic growth.

Some of the differential effects of economic growth have been highlighted by very recent experience. Table 3 shows the changes in the incidence of poverty for selected portions of the population.

TABLE 3

Changes in the Number of Poor, by Age and Sex of Family Head, 1959–67

Status of family head	Number of poor (in millions)			Percentage change
	1959	1967	Change	
Under 65, male	24.5	12.3	−12.2	−50
Under 65, female	8.3	7.7	− 0.6	− 7
Age 65 and over	5.9	5.9	0	0
Total	38.7	25.9	−12.8	−33

Source: Robert A. Levine, "Policy Analysis and Economic Opportunity Programs," in *The Analysis and Evaluation of Public Expenditures: The PPB System*, Vol. 3, Pt. 6: *Analysis and Evaluation in Major Policy Areas: Unresolved Issues and Next Steps*, A Compendium of Papers Submitted to the Subcommittee on Economy in Government of the Joint Economic Committee, 91 Cong. 1 sess. (1969), p. 1189.

Rationale of the Poverty War

The analytical justification for the war on poverty rested on a number of observations about the relationship between economic growth and the decline of poverty. It is a truism that economic growth entails a growth of total income. During periods of growth those poor who are in the labor market, either actually or potentially, find their situations improved by the increased demand for labor services that is a part of economic growth. As growth pro-

[3] "Population Change and Poverty Reduction, 1947–75," in Leo Fishman (ed.), *Poverty amid Affluence* (Yale University Press, 1966), pp. 32, 33.

gresses, more and more of these leave the poverty group. But economic growth does little or nothing for people not connected with the labor market—such as the aged, husbandless mothers, and the handicapped—many of whom are poor.[4] Furthermore, successive increases in median income (which are associated with growth) move an ever smaller tail of the income distribution across a given income level.[5]

Thus it is not surprising that analysis showed that for the postwar period ending in the early 1960s economic growth had apparently become continuously less effective in reducing poverty, and that the incidence of poverty, although declining, was declining at an ever slower rate.[6] The experiences of these decades and the foregoing analysis indicate that, although full employment and sustained economic growth are essential to the elimination of poverty, they are not enough in themselves. Even the 1965–68 period, in which many argued that growth was too fast and employment too high, ended leaving twenty-five million people in poverty. Full employment and rapid growth do not benefit the families with no one in the labor force, with an illiterate family head, or with other characteristics highly correlated with poverty—at least not fast enough.

The government had not been unaware of the existence of the poor. During the Great Depression of the 1930s the federal government had taken on much of the financial burden of caring for them. Most important was the social security legislation, first enacted in 1935 and frequently enlarged through amendment. In addition, expenditures of the Veterans Administration, the Department of Agriculture, and many other agencies have gone and continue to go in part to the poor. The largest of all these measures is

[4] For elaboration of this point, see Lester C. Thurow, "The Causes of Poverty," *Quarterly Journal of Economics,* Vol. 81 (February 1967), pp. 39–57, and his *Poverty and Discrimination* (Brookings Institution, 1969).

[5] This idea, and its mathematics, are developed in W. H. Locke Anderson, "Trickling Down: The Relationship Between Economic Growth and the Extent of Poverty Among American Families," *Quarterly Journal of Economics,* Vol. 78 (November 1964), pp. 511–24.

[6] The experience of the last few years indicates that especially rapid growth, which is associated with considerable inflation, has to some extent halted this decline. A more complete discussion of the value of a "heated up" economy as an antipoverty weapon, even at the risk of inflation, is found in Chap. 5.

the welfare portion of social security, with programs administered by the states but largely financed by the federal government.

By 1961 federal expenditures going to the poor amounted to $9.8 billion. Of this total the main part—$8.3 billion—went as payments under the various welfare provisions of the Social Security Act. The total had increased to $11.9 billion by 1964, still heavily dominated by social security expenditures of $9.8 billion.[7] In a sense this should be thought of as the base from which the war on poverty took off; this sum was not doing the job, in the opinion of those making the decision. They determined to launch the war on poverty in addition to these welfare expenditures. Therefore, an examination of the resource commitment to the poverty war should not focus on totals, which are irrelevant, but on increments beyond this $11.9 billion base.

The Council of Economic Advisers and the Bureau of the Budget were both active in the early planning, no doubt partly because as economists they had become concerned that the growing affluence was passing by a substantial segment of the population, and as budgeteers they were concerned that no one was pulling together all the efforts of various agencies in the poverty area. President John F. Kennedy was clearly intrigued with the idea of a war on poverty, and, after the assassination in November 1963, President Lyndon B. Johnson is reported to have reacted affirmatively to the planning that had gone on to that point; he became a champion of the idea, at least at that time.[8]

The decision was made in early 1964 by President Johnson, affirming the earlier Kennedy commitment, to undertake the war on poverty because, as he said in his message to Congress, "it is right, because it is wise, and because, for the first time in our history, it is possible to conquer poverty." It is clear that the President regarded the proposed agency and statute as new and different additions to the existing arsenal. His message continued:

[7] These are estimates by the Bureau of the Budget of money spent by all federal agencies on poor people. *The Budget of the United States Government, Fiscal Year 1970*, p. 47.

[8] The history of the way in which the Economic Opportunity Act took form is best told in James L. Sundquist, *Politics and Policy: The Eisenhower, Kennedy, and Johnson Years* (Brookings Institution, 1968), Chap. 4.

"The act does not merely expand old programs or improve what is already being done.

"It charts a new course.

"It strikes at the causes, not just the consequences of poverty.

"It can be a milestone in our 180-year search for a better life for our people."[9]

The Economic Opportunity Act was seen by its supporters also as being new and different in two significant ways. First, it was thought to be aimed at the correction of the causes of poverty rather than at the alleviation of symptoms. "Opportunity is our middle name," the poverty warriors were fond of saying. "We don't give handouts," Director Sargent Shriver said on many occasions. By and large this is a valid distinction. Training programs, the teaching of adult literacy, family planning, and most things OEO does or did are directed at making it possible for people to pull themselves out of poverty, whereas most welfare expenditures can only be regarded as relief in one form or another. But the distinction must not be pushed too far; there are remedial programs under other agencies than OEO, such as Medicaid and special educational provisions for disadvantaged areas. These programs have certain aspects of simple relief and are directed at some nonpoor, but it is clear that they are much more than simple relief programs and that they act to eliminate some of the causes of poverty.

Second, the statute embodied a most important coordinating function. The need for this was occasioned by the proliferation of efforts on behalf of the poor, and by the need to have federal agencies working together in the common cause. "I do not intend that the war against poverty become a series of uncoordinated and unrelated efforts. . . . Therefore this bill creates, in the Executive Office of the President, a new Office of Economic Opportunity. Its Director will be my personal chief of staff for the war against poverty." So spoke President Johnson.[10] We shall have occasion to see how this coordination functioned in a later chapter. Here the point to be stressed is that the war against poverty is not the Office of Economic Opportunity and its programs, but the total federal effort, and the concern in this study is correspondingly broad.

[9] *Congressional Record*, Vol. 110, Pt. 4, 88 Cong. 2 sess. (1964), p. 5287.
[10] *Ibid.*, p. 5288.

Analysis of the Act

We turn now to the statute as passed by the Congress in the summer of 1964 and as subsequently amended.[11] The act was passed essentially as submitted in March, by a vote of 226–185 in the House, 61–34 in the Senate. It contained a number of programs, including proposals for community action that gave great administrative latitude to invent new programs. To a certain extent the act was a catchall for various programs that federal agencies had not been able to get Congress to enact or to fund. But there were some unifying threads: it tended to concentrate on youth, with little for the aged, and on education and training. It paid more than lip service to local initiative, and it encouraged or required the poor themselves to assume an important role both in planning and implementing the war at the local level. The heterogeneity will become clear as we look at the provisions of the statute, which dealt with six principal topics: youth programs; community action programs; special antipoverty programs for rural areas; loans for small businesses that could not otherwise obtain credit; work experience programs; and volunteer service and administration. Most of these will be examined in the following sections; however, the community action program, some manpower training, and the administrative aspects will be discussed in later chapters.

Education and Training

There were four programs directed toward either education or training or both: the Job Corps, the Neighborhood Youth Corps, Adult Basic Education, and Work Experience and Training.

[11] The statistical and descriptive data in the remainder of the chapter, unless otherwise noted, are from the Economic Opportunity Act of 1964, 78 Stat. 508, and subsequent amendments and related legislation; U.S. Office of Economic Opportunity, *As the Seed Is Sown*, 4th Annual Report (1969), and preceding annual reports; Office of Economic Opportunity, "A News Summary of the War on Poverty," June 2, 1969, and "OEO Programs, Weekly National Summary," July 14, 1969; *Review of Economic Opportunity Programs*, by the Comptroller General of the United States, 91 Cong. 1 sess. (1969).

JOB CORPS

The Job Corps, designed to help teen-age youth, was primarily a residential program of training and education for young men and women of low-income and otherwise disadvantaged backgrounds. In 1968, 60 percent of the enrollees came from substandard housing.[12] The program was seen by OEO as not only a simple manpower training effort, but as an attempt to engage in human reclamation, in that the corpsmen were considered unlikely to acquire the attitudes and training needed for useful entry into society and the labor market without outside help. In order to give such training and foster such attitudes, the program took these young people from their home environments and kept them for varying periods of time (usually less than a year). The educational part of the program centered on improving skills in reading and arithmetic (corpsmen have had an average reading level from fourth to sixth grade), while training was given in such vocations as automobile mechanics, clerical work, and the use of tools. Health care, personal guidance and counseling, and the away-from-home residential atmosphere were intended to act beneficially on the social attitudes of the corpsmen.

Most Job Corps centers were in rural areas with a conservation flavor (the Civilian Conservation Corps of the 1930s was a clear influence), with 100 to 250 youths in each camp. However, most enrollees (about 60 percent) were in urban centers, the men's centers with from 1,000 to 3,000, the women's centers smaller; at the beginning of fiscal 1969 there were twenty-four urban as against eighty-two rural centers. Six of the urban centers were for men, eighteen for women. There were also three special centers for experimental projects. The conservation centers, as the rural camps are called, are usually operated by agencies of the Interior or Agriculture Department, with OEO funds. The urban centers are run mostly by private corporations—Philco, International Business Machines, Litton Industries, and others—or, in a few instances, by universities. Arrangements with OEO are cost-plus contracts. Recruitment for Job Corps centers is done primarily by state Em-

[12] *Manpower Report of the President, January 1969,* p. 252.

ployment Service agencies for the boys and by a volunteer organization known as WICS (Women in Community Service) for the girls. The Employment Services are also active in placing those who have been through the program.

Corpsmen have stayed for about six months on the average, but many have left before they have benefited to any extent. Many of the dropouts leave in the first month: one principal reason appears to be homesickness, which proves the perceptiveness of John Howard Payne in "Home, Sweet Home." If the first thirty days are disregarded as a trial period, then the number of enrollees who drop out before they are regarded as ready for placement has been in the neighborhood of 15 percent.[13] This does not seem unduly high, given the raw material coming into the system. One can argue that dropout rates should always remain substantially above zero; if they fall too low it indicates that the program is not reaching far enough down for the truly hard-core poor. But there seems to be considerable room for improvement in the selection process, since there are losses from those who drop out early; they have received almost no job-training benefit, while substantial costs are incurred at the time of reporting—medical, clothing, and so on.

There is another aspect of the dropout problem. Job Corps in 1967 and 1968 began enrolling more sixteen-year-olds as the draft and the improving labor markets reduced the pool of applicants at higher ages. These younger enrollees, for understandable reasons, tended to stay for shorter periods, only about four months on the average in 1967. Furthermore, even those who stayed as long as a year were then only seventeen, and many of that age are not ready for meaningful job placement no matter what their training.[14]

All of these things have tended to raise average dropout rates and costs and to depress the placement record. There would seem to be a valid question whether Job Corps really makes sense for youngsters aged sixteen; a committee appointed by the secretary of health, education, and welfare which examined training programs recommended in the spring of 1968 that the age limit be

[13] Job Corps officials believe that a corpsman should remain at least six months to reap the benefits that the program is designed to give.

[14] Sar A. Levitan, *The Great Society's Poor Law: A New Approach to Poverty* (Johns Hopkins Press, 1969), p. 298.

raised to seventeen.[15] The Congress, however, in the 1967 amendments, provided for the admission of those aged fourteen and fifteen, but it required that these participate while living at home.

Job Corps has not been an inexpensive venture. In the beginning it was frequently difficult to know just what the cost of the
program was. Start-up costs tended to dominate at the outset, and
attempts to treat those costs separately were frequently challenged
by a suspicious Congress bent upon demonstrating that the agency
was squandering public funds. The result was that figures like
$15,000 per man/year, and even higher, received public mention.
These figures were unusual, and quickly came down to a level of
$7,500, or $3,500 for the average five-month stint.[16] In addition to
the public outcry about high costs, many communities near Job
Corps centers, fearing riots and Negroes in general, voiced disap-
proval of the program.

A number of changes were written into the statute in 1966
which become more understandable in view of this record. One
was that the director was instructed to see that the average yearly
cost per enrollee in all centers that had been established for more
than nine months be kept at $7,500 per year or less. Another was
that individual center directors were to provide and stringently
enforce "standards of conduct and deportment"[17] and they were
therefore to have power to discipline, including authority to dismiss, subject only to a formal appeal. Before this, the agency had
carefully held the power to dismiss in its own hands; to some extent at least, this authority was compromised by the amendment.
There is doubtful wisdom in such a compromise, since some of the
many center directors have no doubt been tempted to abuse their
authority. A center director's life is easy if he has no problem boys
or girls, but this is a program designed for such young people.

Another amendment in 1966 was also unfortunate, and perhaps
even more significant. The original Job Corps program was for
males only. Over time the agency was pressed, in particular by the

[15] Report of the Committee on Administration of Training Programs (1968) (available from U.S. Department of Health, Education, and Welfare), p. 25.

[16] Glen G. Cain, Benefit/Cost Estimates for Job Corps (University of Wisconsin,
Institute for Research on Poverty, 1967), p. 8. Details on the method are given in
Chap. 7.

[17] 80 Stat. 1453.

congresswomen on the House Committee on Education and Labor (Edith Green and Patsy T. Mink, both strong representatives), to include women and, when that was accomplished, to include more women. This was done by negotiation with OEO's director; by July 1, 1966 there were 2,606 women in a total enrollment of 28,547. Almost all of those directly concerned with the program felt that its real concern should be with males and that additional facilities should be for males, until a much larger dent in the needy male population was made. With marriage and dependency the lot of most females, payoffs to male enrollees would surely be much larger by almost any measure. But such was the power and persuasiveness of two determined committeewomen that when the 1966 legislation was completed, there was a new section in the statute which required the director, by July 1, 1967, to "take such action as may be necessary" to assure that 23 percent of Job Corps enrollees were women.[18] This meant that in fiscal 1967 the number of new spaces for women had to be nearly as large as the number for men—out of a total of roughly 40,000 spaces, over 9,000 had to be for women. In the next year, 1967, the forces of feminism won an even greater victory, with the requirement by statute that 50 per cent female enrollment be achieved as soon as feasible. At times the democratic process in action is a wondrous thing to behold.

By July 1967 Job Corps had built a capacity of over 40,000, and had 32,500 men and 9,500 women actually on board. By July 1969 these numbers had dropped to 13,800 and 5,500, respectively, and fifty-nine of the centers had been closed. The closings were justified by the Department of Labor on the ground that the rural centers were expensive and inefficient. Congressional liberals, believing that the new administration was acting callously toward the poor, protested the closings, to no avail.

The fate of Job Corps is difficult to predict. While the administration promised that many of the rural centers would be replaced by cheaper urban ones, only three of the new centers were in operation in October 1969. It would seem unlikely that the Job Corps will ever regain its 40,000 enrollment. Under the proposed Manpower Training Act of 1969 introduced into Congress in August

---

[18] 80 Stat. 1452, sec. 103.

1969,[19] a wide range of manpower services would be offered to all the poor, including those who would have been eligible for Job Corps. Thus the decline of Job Corps may not spell the end of hope for its target group, but only time will tell.

NEIGHBORHOOD YOUTH CORPS

A second program for teen-age youth was the Neighborhood Youth Corps (NYC), a work-training program designed to serve unemployed boys and girls aged sixteen through twenty-one by providing them with work and some on-the-job training. An in-school component (with a minimum age of fourteen) provided jobs for up to fifteen hours per week at $1.25 to $1.40 per hour, to enable young people to stay in school even when economic pressures were substantial. An out-of-school component was aimed at unemployed dropouts; it supplied jobs for as much as thirty hours per week at up to $1.60 per hour, with an additional ten hours for counseling (often directed at persuading the dropout to return to school), job-readiness training, and sometimes, though not often, some basic education. Finally, summer NYC provided jobs to help needy youngsters remain in school.

The program was delegated by OEO to the Department of Labor. Funds are made available to schools for the in-school component, and to local public or nonprofit bodies—a YMCA, a community action agency, a parks and recreation department—for the out-of-school NYC. Nearly 1,500 local projects have been funded for each year of operation, and more than two million poor youth have been associated with NYC at one time or another. In fiscal year 1969 nearly 500,000 were enrolled. The size of enrollment peaks in the summer. The 1967 amendments to the Economic Opportunity Act added comprehensive programs in work and training for both youth and adults to the manpower package, but NYC retained its separate identity.

For a number of reasons, Neighborhood Youth Corps has had somewhat smoother sailing than Job Corps. At what appears to the general public and their elected representatives a lower cost than Job Corps, it has affected a large number of young people, kept

[19] S. 2838, *Congressional Record,* daily ed., Aug. 12, 1969, pp. S9756–67.

them off the streets, and brought money into local communities.[20] The only major criticism has come in instances where nonpoor have been accepted as enrollees, but eligibility is now strictly enforced.

However, two problems have arisen that disturb enrollees, particularly in connection with the out-of-school NYC projects. One is that many of the projects have been of the make-work or leafraking variety. Young men were quick to perceive this, and the work experience when the job is obviously not a useful one frequently has a negative impact on the boys involved. Substantial numbers have dropped out because of this feature, plus boredom when the job presents no challenge, plus the quite low wages, sometimes as little as $1.25 per hour; a study in the fall of 1966 of 12,500 who terminated indicated that 44 percent left out-of-school NYC for what were called "adjustment problems" and for "other reasons or for whereabouts unknown."[21] That the other 56 percent went on to jobs or further education is impressive, given the nature of the material the program accepts, although many if not most of the 56 percent cannot be considered adequately trained for jobs with a future at the time they leave NYC.

The second problem is more subtle and less visible. It is also shared by Job Corps. It is recruitment, and stems from the similarities and differences of the two programs. In a sense, both have the same aim: to take dropouts, train and motivate them, and make productive citizens of them. But because Job Corps is primarily a residential program, it is more expensive than NYC by a factor of three or more, and it would be an unbelievable coincidence if the two programs happened to be equally effective per dollar of expenditure for all disadvantaged youth entering either program. It would seem obvious that Job Corps ought to be handling the more difficult youngsters and NYC those more nearly employable, but this is not what has occurred. What has happened is partly due to self-selection: a boy or girl applies to Job Corps or to NYC, and is accepted or rejected. There may be some counseling at this point by some recruiters, though in the case of women

---

[20] *Economic Opportunity Amendments of 1967*, S. Rept. 563, 90 Cong. 1 sess. (1967), pp. 14, 20.
[21] *Ibid.*, p. 20.

there are different recruiters, probably competing with one an-other. More important, psychological understanding is not good enough to permit separating with confidence the more difficult from the less difficult. More work ought to be done on this problem, and within present limited capabilities a greater effort should be undertaken to make a sensible distinction at the point of entry between those who ought to go into Job Corps and those who ought to go into Neighborhood Youth Corps.

ADULT EDUCATION

The original statute provided, as a specific item under community action programs, an adult literacy program, directed at people over age eighteen whose basic education was so deficient as to constitute an economic liability. State education agencies were to submit plans to OEO, which would then give grants to the states for stimulating local agencies in setting up instruction programs and demonstration projects, and conducting research on how best to improve adult literacy. From the beginning, the administration of the program was primarily in the hands of the U.S. Office of Education; in 1966 it was removed from the Economic Opportunity Act and its programs transferred to the Department of Health, Education, and Welfare (HEW) by the Adult Education Act of that year.[22]

WORK EXPERIENCE PROGRAMS

Under this head funds for expanding the Aid to Families with Dependent Children (AFDC) program were to be transferred to the Department of Health, Education, and Welfare, which administers AFDC. This is a program directed toward the hard-core unemployed poor, those receiving welfare assistance or eligible for it, and was designed to give work experience and training to those who, for one reason or another, are essentially unemployable in the private sector. Since the start of the program, there have been some 225,000 trainees on the rolls, most of whom entered unskilled, uneducated, and unmotivated. Of these, 80 percent had not completed high school, a fourth had not finished elementary

[22] 80 Stat. 1216.

school, and a third had never held a single job as long as six
months. Through June 1968 projects were operated in fifty-three
states and other civil divisions, many of them in rural areas. Those
enrolled in the projects have been engaged in a variety of activities, almost all quite unskilled, frequently with road commissions,
park services, or recreational facilities.

Appropriations for these activities declined over time. In fiscal
1966, $112 million were spent, in 1967 $100 million, and in 1968
only $42 million. This was accounted for in part by the emergence
of new manpower programs, which gradually absorbed those
served by the work experience programs, and by the desire to shift
the emphasis away from the welfare aspects and toward manpower
aspects. The 1966 amendments to the Economic Opportunity Act
redelegated the manpower parts of the program to the secretary
of labor, effective July 1, 1967; these comprised training, employment counseling, job development, placement, and, where necessary, relocation assistance. HEW continued to be responsible for
pretraining, health, day care, and personal counseling for enrollees
and their families. There appears to have been a basic confusion
about whether this was a welfare or a manpower program; the
rearrangement of responsibilities was an attempt to keep it both,
tilting the balance a bit toward manpower. A further rearrangement was effected by the 1967 amendments to the Social Security
Act, replacing the work experience programs with a work incentive program (WIN). This also is designed for those receiving aid
under AFDC. It is administered by the Department of Labor with
the cooperation of HEW. It became effective July 1, 1968, with a
year of grace for phasing out the earlier programs. Through June
30, 1969, 70,000 welfare recipients had enrolled in WIN. Of these,
1,300 had found jobs that removed them from the welfare rolls.[23]

Loans

The Economic Opportunity Act contained two loan programs, one
for families and cooperatives in rural areas, and one for small businesses in urban areas.

[23] *Washington Post*, Oct. 14, 1969.

RURAL AREA LOANS

This program was designed to assist poor rural families in improving their farms or engaging in other operations to supplement their income. For individuals the maximum loan was first set at $2,500, for a fifteen-year period at an interest rate of 4⅛ percent. The maximum was raised in 1966 to $3,500. Loans were to be made if there was reasonable assurance that repayment could be made and that no other source of credit was available, two provisos which in many cases were inconsistent. Loans to cooperatives were also authorized, with no dollar limit and for a maximum period of thirty years.

By the end of fiscal year 1969, the Department of Agriculture's Farmers Home Administration, to which the program was delegated, had made nearly 53,000 loans to individuals in the amount of $104 million and over 1,400 to rural cooperatives in the amount of $19 million. In 1968, 47 percent of the new borrowers in the South were Negroes. The typical family receiving a loan had an income below $2,000 for family living expenses. Nearly 60 percent of the loan recipients were over forty years of age.

This program is something of an anomaly even within the context of the already heterogeneous Economic Opportunity Act and was probably included because it was felt that something had to be provided for rural America. It was a loan rather than a grant program so that it would be attractive to the Congress, but it has been argued that if the loans could be repaid they had been made to the wrong people. It is, furthermore, difficult to believe that loans of the size indicated could do much to reduce rural poverty, and insofar as the program had any tendency to keep in rural areas poor people who would otherwise have moved away, the program perhaps actually did a disservice.

The impact of these negative factors was such that OEO at one time recommended to the Bureau of the Budget that the program be dropped. The reasoning was that it tended to anchor to the land submarginal people—those who would otherwise have moved away—while many poor people who would have stayed anyway would face an extremely difficult problem of repaying the loans in the not too distant future. The picture of the federal government foreclosing on large numbers of very poor farmers is not an attractive one, yet wholesale forgiveness of outstanding loans would be anathema to the purposes of the war on poverty.

The recommendation did not stand (and if it had, probably the Bureau of the Budget would not have accepted it). OEO reversed itself on several grounds. First, the program was not very expensive —some $30 million annually. Second, it was getting to the hard-core poor and to Negroes, and incidentally reintroducing the Department of Agriculture to the really poor after thirty years.[24] Third, most of the loans were going to older people, who would not move in any case. On balance, therefore, it was reaching into rural America; and while the program was far from perfect, it did not appear to be having a negative impact, and no one could figure out a better way to get to the rural poor. The repayment problem is a real one, and it is not clear how it will be met.

LOANS TO SMALL BUSINESS

In its original form this program provided that the Small Business Administration should orient some of its activity and loan funds toward the poor and that OEO should provide advice to small businesses so helped. The loan funds, in other words, were SBA's, the administration and advice were paid for by OEO. In the words of OEO, "A major purpose of the program, besides increasing the productivity and income of the borrowers, is to provide the community-building factor of locally-owned businesses in poverty-stricken neighborhoods and to open up the opportunity of business ownership to minority groups to whom it has often been closed."[25]

This took the concrete form in 1965 of Small Business Development Centers (SBDCs) in urban areas where loans were arranged and advice provided, largely through volunteers from the world of successful business. SBDCs were established in forty-six communities in twenty-four states and the District of Columbia at the peak, so that coverage was never very substantial.

From the start the program suffered from not knowing what it

---

[24] Loans to poor farmers were part of the New Deal program in the 1930s.

[25] U.S. Office of Economic Opportunity, *Congressional Presentation* (March 1966), p. 73.

was supposed to be doing. Initially, those eligible for loans were those whose income was below that required to meet basic needs, which was not otherwise defined, or those who would employ poor persons. The maximum loan was set at $25,000. Because of the looseness of the eligibility definition, loans were made at a rapid rate and available funds were threatened with exhaustion; at the same time it became apparent that loans were consistently going to those with incomes substantially above the poverty line.

Since the loan program was assumed to be a part of the poverty program, OEO viewed this development with concern. It argued that these funds should go to the poor; SBA argued that if eligibility was restricted to the poor, reputable applicants could not be found. A compromise was reached and on November 15, 1965, eligibility was redefined to include those whose income was below the poverty line plus $1,500. At the same time the maximum loan was reduced to $15,000.

The effect of these changes was to bring the program to a halt. The SBA field offices claimed there were no applicants; OEO suspected a strike against the new rules. This was a classic case of the conflict between the desire of OEO to direct funds to the poor and of an established agency to direct funds to those easier to work with. It is interesting that black pressure at the time was on SBA's side; this was at the very beginning of the emergence of the idea of black capitalism and ghetto self-determination. Blacks wanted money for black businessmen in the ghettos. They were beginning to develop the rub-off theory—the give-us-the-tools-and-we'll-solve-our-own-poverty notions that have flowered since.

The OEO at the time was lukewarm about the whole idea of loans, particularly loans as small as the program contemplated. The fear was that such loans would enable recipients in ghettos to begin small restaurants, or hair-dressing establishments, retail shops of one sort or another. Not only can such places survive only if the proprietor and his family put in long hours (and not account properly for their labor input), but those that did succeed would simply drive a competitor out of business. Changing the names and creditors of such enterprises hardly seemed an effective way to fight poverty.

Accordingly, it is not surprising that OEO lost even more interest in the program as a poverty weapon when the next compromise moved the eligibles substantially up the income scale. On March 3, 1966, eligibility was defined as encompassing those at the poverty line plus $2,500, with the further proviso that up to 20 percent of the loans could be made without reference to this standard, provided the applicant would use the proceeds in some sort of disadvantaged area.

In late 1966 the program was transferred in its entirety to the Small Business Administration, without objection from OEO. The poverty agency had concluded that, whatever its merits on other grounds, it was not worth the effort as part of the poverty arsenal. SBA changed the emphasis to opportunity loans, stressing the idea that some businessmen lacked opportunities to borrow, presumably because of racial discrimination, and set out to plug that gap without reference to the income of the borrowers.

The irony is the subsequent emergence, as part of the black power thrust, of the concept of black capitalism, which was espoused by Senators Robert Kennedy and Jacob Javits as well as by many black leaders. In this SBA loans could be quite helpful, and the argument that these loans may not help the poverty population directly loses some, though not all, of its force. Its aim could be thought of as being redirected toward helping Negro ownership of enterprises, now thought of as a good thing in itself, whether it raised poverty incomes or not. Even on these grounds, however, there is reason to question whether these small loans really increase the general welfare in the ghetto. Although the program serves the laudable end of giving loans to people (notably minority groups) who might otherwise be unable to get them, and thus generally stimulates small business, it is not a poverty program, and its successes and failures are only marginally relevant to the war on poverty.

Other OEO Programs

The Economic Opportunity Act also included a program to give some help to migrant workers and a program to give volunteers an opportunity to offer assistance to the poor.

MIGRANT WORKERS

The condition of migrant and other seasonally employed workers has constituted a particularly repellent chapter in the history of American poverty. These workers and their families number some seven million persons, most of them "enjoying" an average income of less than $2,000 per family per year. By and large they have had almost no social services available to them—indeed, they are often specifically excluded because of residence requirements.

The Economic Opportunity Act included programs to help these people, although only some $25 million per year were allocated to them, less than $4 per migrant. There are state programs in a few states—for example, California—and local programs in others; in 1968 programs were operated in thirty-five states through ninety-five public and private agencies. Programs usually provide child care for workers' children, education for both the parents and the children, sanitary facilities in migrant camps, the construction of temporary and permanent housing, and health and legal services. In some projects there is strong emphasis on retraining the migrant worker for a new and better vocation.[26] It is clear that the problem of the migrant worker remains a huge one and that, as is the case with so many of OEO's programs, resources thus far expended, while accomplishing some good, have barely begun to scratch the surface.

VISTA

The Volunteers in Service to America (VISTA), sometimes known as the domestic Peace Corps, was established to assist in programs to combat poverty. It is composed of private citizens and

[26] In one such program, which concerned only six workers, the expense of $1,000 for the training program was returned to the federal government in less than a year through increased tax revenues from the men retrained. While successes of this nature are far more spectacular than the norm, they show what OEO is generally trying to do—make a group of fairly useless people into members of the economy who will be able to pay their own way. Seen in this light, the war on poverty is anything but charity—it is an investment in future gross national product and federal, state, and local revenues.

in one sense is a bridge between middle-class America and the poor. The volunteers live among the poor twenty-four hours a day, helping them in innumerable ways. The great bulk (87 percent in late 1967) have been involved in one way or another with OEO-related programs—in migrant camps, on Indian reservations, in neighborhood centers, and so on.[27] In some rural areas, where leadership is so characteristically lacking, they have been instrumental in helping develop community action program applications.

Volunteers normally give one year of service, although about 25 percent have reenlisted for a second year and another 9 percent stayed some months beyond their one-year stint.[28] At the end of May 1969 they numbered 4,400, at an annual cost of about $30 million. More than half of the volunteers are in urban areas, 35 percent in rural areas, 3 percent in Job Corps centers as counselors, and 3 percent in mental health programs.

The question whether this allocation makes sense might be raised. VISTA personnel should be used where their unique characteristics can be most useful. The most important of these characteristics is a willingness to work without reference to the clock. On an Indian reservation, for example, they are on duty all the time, not for forty hours a week. This, combined with a presumed special compassion for the poor, means that they can perform assignments for which it is not possible to hire an employee. Perhaps this argues for an even greater assignment to rural areas, where poverty resources have such difficulty penetrating. It surely argues against using members of VISTA in mental retardation programs unless the persons in these programs can be brought back, at least partly, into society through the efforts of the volunteers. Initially, there was some misuse of this kind. Efforts are now directed toward mental health. The basic problem in assessing the performance of VISTA is the difficulty in specifying, let alone quantifying, just what it is that the volunteers are supposed to be doing.

One other aspect of VISTA deserves brief mention. From time to time the volunteers have been accused of fomenting social un-

---

[27] *Economic Opportunity Amendments of 1967*, S. Rept. 563, 90 Cong. 1 sess. (1967), p. 70.
[28] *Ibid.*

rest, of organizing rent strikes, of picketing welfare agencies, and
the like. No doubt there was some of this. No doubt also there
should be some of this. There is a fine line here which is difficult if
not impossible to draw. Many VISTA members are young and
idealistic, and one reason they joined the corps was to take part in
eliminating injustice. At times the only way to accomplish this was
by defying a local or state law, and many did not flinch when this
appeared to be necessary. Mistakes and errors of judgment no
doubt were made; even without these their actions were sometimes unpopular with the powers that be. This is but one of the
things that has kept life lively in the Office of Economic Opportunity.

Other New Legislation

The financial dimensions of the war on poverty are indicated in
Table 4. Through 1963, the year before the new program began,
essentially all of these expenditures were ameliorative, designed to
make the lot of the poor more bearable. Much, though by no
means all, of the increase in later years purports to attack the causes
of poverty, to make people or communities better, to make it pos-

TABLE 4

Federal Aid to the Poor, Selected Years, 1961–69

(Fiscal years, in billions of current dollars)

Category	1961	1964	1968	1969[a]
Education	0.1	0.1	2.3	2.2
Employment assistance	0.1	0.2	1.6	2.0
Health assistance	0.7	1.0	4.1	5.0
Income assistance	8.3	9.8	12.4	12.9
Other maintenance assistance	0.5	0.7	1.3	1.9
Total	9.8	11.9	21.7	24.0

Source: *The Budget of the United States Government, Fiscal Year 1970*, p. 47. Figures are rounded and will not
necessarily add to totals. It is well to stress that these sums are only those reaching the poor. Health expenditures, for example, were much higher than $4.1 billion in 1968; of the total expended, the poor received $4.1
billion.
   a. Estimated.

sible for people to work themselves out of poverty. The distinction is important: it is the second type of expenditure that was to be the backbone of the war on poverty.

The largest exception to this generalization was Medicare, enacted in 1965 as an amendment to the Social Security Act. Essentially, Medicare alone accounts for the rapid growth in the row called "Health" in the table; it embraces all those over sixty-five, not just the poor, but it makes a major contribution to the well-being of the poor and will no doubt contribute heavily to keeping many of the aged nonpoor from falling into poverty because of large medical expenditures. To some extent Medicare will make it possible for some older people to hold jobs who otherwise could not, but essentially its purpose is not to cure poverty among the aged. The beneficial effects that it will have, both in enabling some poor to work and in preventing many aged from becoming poor, however, give Medicare an important role in the war on poverty.[29]

Medicaid, on the other hand, also part of the Social Security Amendments of 1965, is directed at all "medically indigent," regardless of age. Under this provision, each state is to set up a medical assistance program which will be awarded grants by the Department of Health, Education, and Welfare. The authorizing legislation requires that medical assistance be provided "for all Federally aided public assistance recipients (the aged, blind, disabled, and families with dependent children)" as well as for other medically needy people, such that "by 1975, states must be providing medical assistance to all who cannot afford the care they need—whether recipients of public assistance or not."[30] The provision is not yet fully effective, but it appears that many states will define medical indigency at income levels substantially above the federal government's poverty level. To the extent that this is done, some Medicaid expenditures will go to the nonpoor, although it is likely that these expenditures will enable marginal nonpoor to stay above the poverty line. Any definition of medical indigence is almost bound to include all those below the poverty line, and

[29] Payments made under Medicare are not counted as income when determining a family's status as poor or nonpoor.

[30] U.S. Office of Economic Opportunity, *Catalog of Federal Assistance Programs* (1967), p. 320.

those expenditures that do go to the poor should be instrumental in helping to cure poverty rather than simply ameliorating it.

The increase in federal expenditures on education for the poor is in large part a reflection of the impact of the Elementary and Secondary Education Act of 1965, which includes a provision for funds to improve the quality of public education in economically deprived areas. This is one of the government's weapons in the attack on the link between low incomes and poor education. Its effectiveness is no doubt limited by the requirement that the funds be funneled through the states, which means that in many states they get to the wrong places or are used for the wrong purposes.

Chapter 4 includes discussion at greater length of the problems associated with the improvement of public education for the poor, and it will be seen there that administrative difficulties are only a part of the problems associated with the way in which the moneys are spent. The legislative establishment of the principle that federal money should be used to assist deprived schools is very important, however. Whatever solution to the problem of the high correlation between poverty and poor education may be found will require money to be effective. Without the aid of such federal funds as those provided in this act, there could be little or no hope for the kind of improvement that is so sorely needed.

The work and training increases in Table 4 come largely from new programs like Job Corps and Neighborhood Youth Corps and a reorientation of the programs operated under the Manpower Development and Training Act. This act was originally passed in 1962 to retrain skilled workers whose skills had become obsolete. In 1966, by administrative directive, the program changed its emphasis so that two-thirds of its effort was directed at training the poor.[31] All of these manpower programs will be treated more fully in Chapter 5, which is devoted to manpower policy, an area clearly critical to the war on poverty.

The figures in Table 4 make it clear that the Economic Opportunity Act has by no means dominated the war on poverty in a fiscal sense. Nevertheless, the administration clearly regarded it as something quite special and new; it is not too much to say that it

[31] *Manpower Report of the President,* March 1966, p. 3.

was thought of as the heart of the program. It established a new agency whose director, partly because of his own personality but partly for statutory reasons, became the President's chief of staff for the war on poverty.

In this chapter we have briefly reviewed some of the operative provisions of the Economic Opportunity Act of 1964. Changes in the statute not mentioned here will be described later as the history of some of the more important programs is discussed and analyzed. These changes were minor for the most part until 1967 when basic modifications to the act were legislated; these will also be discussed in some detail. Despite the modifications, however, throughout the years since the passage of the original act the central position of OEO and its director in the war on poverty have remained intact.

CHAPTER IV

The Community Action Program

The familiar community action program authorized by Title II-A
is clearly the most important part of the Economic Opportunity Act: it uses roughly half of OEO's annual appropriation; it
has been at the heart of most of the controversy that swirls around
the war on poverty; it is the only truly novel aspect of the war;
and it is a highly complex and widely misunderstood concept.[1] It
is not easy to find two people who agree on what community action either is or should be.

The antecedents are to be found in the Ford Foundation's gray
areas projects and in the activities of the President's Committee on
Juvenile Delinquency and Youth Crime.[2] Both of these were
started in the early 1960s in an attempt to find alternatives to urban renewal as the major weapon to be used for improving the
situation in the American slum. Both programs had as a philosophical justification the notion that antisocial behavior on the

---

[1] The statistical and descriptive data in this and the following paragraphs, unless
otherwise noted, are from the Economic Opportunity Act of 1964, 78 Stat. 508, and
subsequent amendments and related legislation; U.S. Office of Economic Opportunity,
As the Seed Is Sown, 4th Annual Report (1969), and preceding annual reports; Office
of Economic Opportunity, "A News Summary of the War on Poverty," June 2, 1969,
and "OEO Programs, Weekly National Summary," July 14, 1969; *Review of Economic
Opportunity Programs,* by the Comptroller General of the United States, 91 Cong.
1 sess. (1969).

[2] The best account of these experiments is found in Peter Marris and Martin Rein,
Dilemmas of Social Reform: Poverty and Community Action in the United States
(Atherton, 1967). The gray areas projects take their name from the deteriorating city
areas that lie between downtown and the suburbs.

part of the urban poor, particularly juvenile delinquents, could be understood as a reaction on the part of such people to a society which used middle-class standards of success but which provided them little or no opportunity for the achievement of that success. The solution was to change the environment in which the disadvantaged lived so as to improve the quality of their opportunities. Furthermore, it was felt that community action, unlike urban renewal, for example, would be able to deal with all of the problems affecting the poor at once, and be able to do so at the local level. The key then to the gray areas projects and the President's committee was the idea of local coordination and control of all possible resources, both public and private, that could be employed to improve the environment of the urban poor. These two programs, and the concept of community action found in them, had enough promise to persuade the framers of the Economic Opportunity Act that they should be greatly expanded. Thus expanded, they have become the heart of the poverty war—the community action program.

Definition of Community Action

The basic statute and the amendments of 1967 have given a fairly specific definition of community action.[3] There are four principal attributes to a community action program (CAP), and each of these deserves careful examination. First, it is a program which "mobilizes and utilizes resources, public or private, of any urban or rural" area in an attack on poverty. There is, then, the idea of bringing the community's resources to bear on poverty in some fashion that had not been done before. The local community would be central to the program and would be exercising its own initiative. Most urban community action programs, as they have been developed, cover no more than a city, and typically less; rural areas are likely to be larger, perhaps a county or several counties.

Second, a community action program "provides services, assistance, and other activities of sufficient scope and size to give promise of progress toward elimination of poverty or a cause or causes

[3] 78 Stat. 516, 81 Stat. 690.

of poverty through developing employment opportunities, improving human performance, motivation, and productivity, or bettering the conditions under which people live, learn, and work." Here the points to notice are the emphasis on the provision of services and the idea that both people and environments need improvement and can benefit from it.

Third, community action is to be aimed at "the strengthening of community capabilities for planning and coordinating Federal, State, and other assistance related to the elimination of poverty." As will be seen, the programs ideally provide much more than services specifically enumerated within the text. They are designed to make known and available to residents of a given target area all of the services to which they are entitled, and further to make such programs "more responsive to local needs and conditions." The vehicle provided by the statute for "planning, conducting, administering and evaluating a community action program" is the community action agency, or CAA. Originally this was to be "a public or private nonprofit agency (other than a political party), or a combination thereof." Under the amendments of 1967, the CAA must be "a State or political subdivision of a State . . . or a public or private nonprofit agency or organization which has been designated by a State or such a political subdivision."[4] The difference is important, as it forces a closer liaison between the CAA and the local government, a liaison that is strengthened by the 1967 provision that one-third of the CAA governing board must be made up of public officials or their representatives. The new provisions emphasize that CAAs are not federal establishments and their employees are not federal employees. The relationship between OEO and CAAs is financial only; control is in no sense direct.

It was the expectation of the backers of this 1967 amendment that cities or other political subdivisions would largely replace the typical CAA, which up to that time had been a private nonprofit agency. The politics of the amendment revolved around the ques-

[4] Any political subdivision or group of subdivisions of a state may opt to have its own CAA, rather than be a part of the CAA of a larger subdivision within the state hierarchy of administrative districts. In other words, while the statute now requires that local governments be a part of CAA, each government of each political subdivision of a state may have an independent CAA if it so desires.

tion of how much power "city hall" should have. In fact, however, very few CAAs have been changed as a result of the amendment.

Finally, community action is to be "developed, conducted, and administered with the maximum feasible participation of residents of the areas and members of the groups served." This is one of the most famous phrases in the statute and has generated continuous controversy. It is fascinating that its inclusion in the statute appears to have been without either opposition or even notice in 1964. Furthermore, although its import may have changed, the phrase "maximum feasible participation of residents" remains intact in the 1967 amendments. It is this provision that has led to the participation of the poor in the administration and conduct of programs after they have been funded and developed.

Representation of the Poor

One issue that developed immediately was the meaning of "maximum feasible participation," particularly with relation to membership of the boards of directors. The OEO felt its way on the issue, insisting at first only that there be some representation, but gradually moved toward the idea that the appropriate number was somewhere between a quarter and a third, on the average. Some boards might have only poor members; this was particularly likely for the CAAs on Indian reservations. The agency also tolerated, at least in the beginning, substantially less than a quarter from the groups served. This was the case, for example, if a prospective CAA had a good plan and promised to add poor members in the near future. The issue was resolved in the 1966 amendments by a requirement that by March 1, 1967, representation of poor people in the areas served should make up at least one-third of the membership of all CAA boards. This provision is retained in the 1967 amendments, and the phrase "maximum feasible," whatever its hortatory value, has come to mean one-third.

The provision assured that a formerly inarticulate group would now have representation on an agency making plans for a community, and, more important, disbursing funds. In many areas—particularly in the South, where there were racial implications, but

by no means only in the South—this presented a new and un-
known challenge to local officials. Not unnaturally conflicts
emerged in some areas, and in a few they still go on. Partly this is
because no one really knew what the poor representatives were
supposed to do. Were they simply there to assure that their inti-
mate knowledge of poverty would make planning more realistic,
or were they there, as some insisted, to bring about basic institutional change? Some thought and acted one way, some the other.
There was no general pattern in all urban and rural communities,
and none should have been expected.

This is an important issue. Many thoughtful people regarded
community action essentially as a vehicle for social change or, if
institutions refused to change without it, social revolution. There
has been a broad spectrum of both thought and action with regard
to the role of the CAA in institution changing. Urban slums do
need institutional change; almost by definition slums are a perver-
sion of American institutions. Many CAAs have brought change
which all would applaud; for example, the public Employment
Service in many areas has moved into neighborhood centers in poverty areas for the first time. In other areas CAAs have obtained a
voice in making rules about tenants in public housing. In still others, CAA lawyers providing free legal services have sued the welfare agency to enjoin reductions in welfare payments. CAAs have
also attempted change which some would not applaud. They have
manned and organized picket lines around city hall protesting local ordinances. It has been alleged that in Newark poverty workers
encouraged the 1967 riots.[5]

It is not clear where one would ideally draw the line on institution changing. The original statute was mute on the point, unless
stress on "the opportunity to live in decency and dignity" is regarded as encouraging the process. Many on the left have regarded any accommodation with the powers that be as capitula-
tion, and this made, in the early days, for almost warlike confron-
tations in such cities as Syracuse, San Francisco, and Newark. The
1967 amendments, requiring that the CAA be a political subdivision of a state, or be approved by one, made it explicit that a fed-

[5] *New York Times,* July 19, 1969.

eral agency would not be allowed consciously to employ federal funds to foster social revolution. By and large, however, the amendments drew the line on institution changing rather farther to the right than many would have had it, including a number of the original high-ranking officers of OEO. The basic question that the CAAs still have to face is how fast they can go in nudging their communities toward desirable change. The 1967 amendments, requiring CAAs and governments to be part and parcel of one another, have decreased friction, but they have also slowed the nudging process; in fact, this is what they were designed to do. Those responsible for the change preferred control and predictability to spontaneity and reform. Due to a lack of funds, it has never been clear how productive the CAAs could be in pushing for reform, but now, because of the statutory requirement, it is almost certain that they will be less so.

In an interesting and highly publicized new book, Daniel P. Moynihan reaches the verdict that, in the words of his Chapter 7 title, "Community Action Loses."[6] In tracing the history, and more notably what he regards as the failures, of CAP, Moynihan substantiates the assertion made earlier in this chapter that no two persons share the same conception of what community action is or should be. He condemns CAP largely because it has not brought about institutional change, but he fails to credit amply all of the other complex functions (notably the provision of services) that are in the program and that have been outlined. Thus his concept of community action differs from the one presented here.

In part this results from what seems to be his concentration on the experience of only a few cities at an early period in CAP's history.[7] In addition, there is more to community action than the fomenting of social change through participatory democracy. To conclude that the program loses because of failure in this area alone is to condemn on grounds that are too narrow.

Finally, although there has been noise rather than substance in

[6] *Maximum Feasible Misunderstanding: Community Action in the War on Poverty* (Free Press, 1969).

[7] Although Moynihan's book appeared in 1969, it is based on a lecture series given in 1967, which was in turn based on an article that appeared in the preceding year: "What Is 'Community Action'?" *The Public Interest* (Fall 1966), pp. 3–8.

too many cases, a recent study shows that CAP has clearly had an impact on local institutions in many areas, an impact that has shifted power toward the poor.[8]

In the conclusion to his book Moynihan observes that "it remains to be seen whether it [participation of the poor] can do what is promised for it." This is certainly true, and the final evaluation will have to wait on time and a more comprehensive definition of what is promised than is presented in Moynihan's book, or in this. Moynihan has since entered the Nixon administration as adviser to the President on urban problems; in that position he has used his influence to keep CAP alive, so that there may in time be sufficient data to facilitate an appraisal of CAP in the broad perspective of experience.

A Model CAA

What would an ideal comprehensive CAA be like in an urban area? It would be run by a board of directors numbering perhaps thirty-five (not more than fifty-one). Twelve would be public officials (the mayor, people from the county, the school boards, and perhaps the public health service) unless "the number of such officials reasonably available or willing to serve is less than one-third of the membership of the board."[9] Somewhat more than twelve (at least one-third) would be poor and live in the target areas, with some representation of the poor from each target area administered by the CAA. These might have been elected but more likely would have been picked by ministers, social workers, or others who know the area and the people. The statute requires merely that these representatives be chosen "in accordance with democratic selection procedures adequate to assure that they are representative of the poor in the area served." The roster would be completed by a number of outstanding private citizens, representative of the major groups and interests in the community that

[8] Barss, Reitzel, and Associates, *Community Action and Institutional Change,* An Evaluation Prepared for the Office of Economic Opportunity (Cambridge, Mass.: Barss, Reitzel, 1969).

[9] 81 Stat. 693.

could be brought to bear on the program (as business, labor, industry, and religious leaders).

There would be a number of neighborhood centers, at least one for each "target area"—the geographical area to be served by the CAA. The target area is defined in the charter creating the CAA or in the initial application to OEO for funds. It is always a low income area, but not all of its residents are below the poverty line. Sometimes a CAA has several target areas under its jurisdiction, not necessarily contiguous. Each neighborhood center would contain a number of general counselors, an Employment Service placement officer, a youth counseling service, a legal services office, some sort of health clinic, a recreation hall, a child care center, and a number of neighborhood workers and their supervisor. These last are "outreach" people, poor themselves and residents of the area. They serve as contacts with the people in the area in many situations. For example, employers in some cities notify the appropriate neighborhood center whenever a resident resigns his job. The outreach person makes a call to try to find out why he quit and whether he needs some available service.

In addition to providing these services and personnel, the centers would be in close touch with the school system, the welfare agency, the Manpower Administration, the local draft board, the public housing agency, and so on. They would frequently intercede with one of these agencies on behalf of a poor person, and they might very well lobby at a city council meeting or with the public officials on the CAA board for or against an ordinance that bore on the welfare of the poor. They would become, in short, the voice of the poor in the area. In line with community action's role as a coordinator as well as a provider of services, their funding would come from many sources, not simply from OEO. The Employment Service man or men, for example, would be on the state labor department payroll.

In dispensing services, the CAA or neighborhood center would have matters of eligibility to consider. Anyone would be entitled to seek counseling or to use the recreation facilities. But a person seeking family planning services, or legal assistance, or a spot in a Job Corps center would have to meet the criteria specified in the law or the regulations. These sometimes differ from program to program, but the general requirement is that the applicant be poor as measured by the income standards described in Chapter 2.

Existing community action agencies are in very different stages of maturity, with few if any of them in the ideal state outlined above. Of the more than 1,000 CAAs operating in 1969, many were so-called single component CAAs. These agencies originally applied for and received funds to run only one program, such as Head Start. Some of these subsequently became comprehensive; those that did not are hardly fulfilling the purpose of community action. Some CAAs are merely in the process of making an initial application to Washington. They have a program development grant from OEO which enables them to hire a minimal staff, perhaps contract for planning help with a local university, and begin preparing an application containing a plan for their own local war on poverty. The national office offers some help in this process by providing printed guidelines telling the community what kind of financial support it can expect and what sorts of programs have appeared to be successful in other communities. Help can be obtained from the state technical assistance office; most states have grants from OEO to establish such a staff. There is also an OEO regional office (there are seven of these), which will sometimes send a staff member to help. But essentially—and this is the important point—the preparation of the application and whatever plan is behind it has been considered a local responsibility. The local people are assumed to know their own problems best, as well as their own resources and gaps. In considering the application, OEO's national or regional office has done a minimum of second-guessing of the local community. OEO's prime concern has been that the application conforms with the law. This local initiative has been eroded away, but it is important to realize how central to the concept it originally was.

The national or regional office also provides extensive advisory services to individual CAAs. It issues guides explaining what can be applied for and how best to apply, and presses those programs (so-called national emphasis or special emphasis programs) which are funded on the national level and, being outside the community's quota, are "free" to the individual CAA. Guides are also issued describing what is working well in other communities, giving legal advice, and serving a host of functions that make the national office, among other things, a clearinghouse for useful information. While OEO can urge that serious consideration be given to components of the war on poverty that it regards as particularly valuable, in the last analysis it lets the community decide—in this respect there *is* local initiative on a substantial scale.

The national office performs one other important function: it takes action in situations where a CAA is remiss in discharging its duties. There have been occasions when an established CAA obtained funding and then refused to include among its programs and planners the "legitimate" aspirations of one or more local groups. In such cases the national office was faced with a decision whether to fund a new group, thereby establishing a competitor to the existing CAA. Where this was done, it was for the purpose of ensuring that established and conservative local groups did not gain control of the funds for the war on poverty and block out reform groups.

Changes and Limitations

Passage of the 1967 amendments made it less certain that the forces of change would win out. The framers of the amendments intended that this be the case and insured it in two ways.[10] For one, the local CAA would be closer to the state government hierarchy, and it would thus be more difficult for purely political reasons to interfere with it. Added to this was the provision that the OEO director could not fund a new group without at least the tacit consent of the governor of the state. The use of poverty money was thus more likely to become a question of political patronage within the state. It is still possible for the national office to fund a new group if it is determined to do so, but the roadblocks created by the 1967 amendments make what was always a difficult decision

[10] In passing the amendments, the Congress was clearly reacting to severe political pressure from back home.

even more difficult, and local initiative has come closer to meaning the initiative of the local government, which can be at variance with what the community may desire.

In addition to a political erosion of local initiative, there has also taken place a corresponding change in the fiscal position of the CAAs. For the first two years the authorization legislation indicated amounts of money to be spent by title of the act only, and the appropriation legislation merely provided a lump sum for OEO as a whole. This meant that a lump sum authorization was made for all the community action programs. For about six months of fiscal 1965, this amounted to $340 million, and for all of fiscal 1966, $850 million. In a statutory sense, these funds could be spent on any of the many varied programs that were not specified but that came under the very general language of CAP. The agency set aside some funds for research, for program development, for experimentation and demonstration, and so on, but the bulk of the funds were available for allocation to various programs in accordance with the applications made by local communities.

In early 1965 the first of what came to be called special emphasis programs was devised—the very successful (perhaps more accurately, very popular) Head Start, a program to give preschool children of poor families experience needed to catch up with those better off. In the budget request for fiscal 1966 the agency asked for $630 million for CAP, of which $179 million was to be used for Head Start. This was a figure determined in Washington, not by the plans of the communities. Thus the amount of local initiative money was diminished by taking the $179 million out of the total pot. The Head Start money became "free" to the communities; if they turned down the program they simply lost that money. Under these circumstances the program was not turned down. Without such treatment of Head Start as a national emphasis program, it is possible that many communities would have chosen about the same amount of Head Start money as they actually received. There is no intent to imply here that the mix of programs that developed was inferior. The point is that local initiative was narrowed.

The example set with Head Start was emulated by OEO with the free legal services program and with Upward Bound, a program to get poor youngsters qualified for and into college. These differed only in that each was less expensive and hence encroached less on local initiative. But the pattern was clear: less money for local agencies to allocate.

In 1966, something new was added as Congress decided to enter the earmarking business. CAP was amended by the addition of several sections, specifying that OEO would carry out programs on Head Start, legal services, comprehensive health services, emergency loans to individuals, and job training at a subprofessional level. These were all programs that heretofore had not been mentioned, and mention was not required in the statute to permit them to be implemented—the breadth of the language was ample. Furthermore, OEO had every intention of pressing forward with most of the enumerated programs, and Congress knew this.

Why then the writing of the new sections? It permitted the Congress to earmark funds for specific items in CAP. The 1966 amendments authorized $846 million for fiscal 1967 for community action and, within that authorization, set aside definite amounts for each section (by number) for which it wished to itemize. This froze each of these favored programs into the statute, along with its money.[11] The extent of reallocation that earmarking brought about is impossible to specify, since it is not known what the communities would have chosen if they had had a free choice, but again the resulting inflexibility was substantial. Of the $846 million authorized, $323 million was left after the designations had been made.

In the 1967 amendments the Congress greatly increased its scope for earmarking.[12] The statute required that there be eight special (national) emphasis programs—Head Start, Follow Through, legal services, comprehensive health services, Upward Bound, emergency food and medical services, family planning, and senior opportunities and services. It was only because the authorizations

---

[11] Earmarking by Congress was not limited to CAP. Specific amounts were designated for Job Corps and Neighborhood Youth Corps, and a new Special Impact program was added (together with funds for it) to employ residents of poverty-stricken urban areas in improving their own neighborhoods. It was earmarking for specific programs within CAP that was new in 1966.

[12] The reader will recognize the analogy to the well-known congressional preference for categorical grants as opposed to block grants.

and appropriations committees could not get together on earmarking for 1968 that some discretion was left to the director in that year. Overall, however, it is clear that the 1967 amendments contributed to a loss in the flexibility of CAP, and that local initiative, which is presumed to rank just below motherhood on the political scale of values, was further circumscribed.[13]

Special Emphasis Programs

Thus far in this chapter we have explored at some length the legislation that makes community action a central part of the war on poverty. We have noted some of the philosophical justifications underlying community action, especially the idea that environments need improvement and that an invaluable aid to the realization of that improvement is an indigenous planning and coordinating agency—the CAA. Because of legislative amendments to the Economic Opportunity Act of 1964, the operative meaning of CAP has been changed: the original emphasis on local planning has not been lost, but the practice of local planning has been limited by earmarking for the special emphasis programs[14] which use more than half of all CAP funds, and the meaning of local planning has been changed by the specifications concerning the membership of CAA boards. Later in this chapter we shall discuss how

[13] There is an interesting sidelight to this move for earmarking. It started in the summer of 1966 among the Democrats on the House Subcommittee on the War on Poverty Program of the Committee on Education and Labor. Following hearings, the markup of the bill was done by the Democratic members, who then presented it to the full committee, which voted it out; the Republicans played essentially no role. The Democratic members of the subcommittee were liberals who might have been expected to support the administration position and to oppose earmarking. Among them, for example, were James H. Scheuer of New York, Sam M. Gibbons of Florida, John Brademas of Indiana, and Patsy T. Mink of Hawaii. In order, so it was said, to pour oil on the troubled political waters of the poverty program, the earmarking was imposed (as were the requirements to have a minimum number of women in the Job Corps), changing rather basically the nature of the legislation. Adam Clayton Powell, who was chairman of both the full committee and the subcommittee, attended sessions only when there seemed a good likelihood of publicity, and did not participate in the markup.

[14] Special emphasis programs are only *funded* from Washington; each CAA still draws up a local plan to fit the national program to its special needs.

CAP can and does operate in confronting some of the problems of poverty not covered by the special emphasis programs. Here we will look briefly at three of the national programs that seem likely to give the flavor of how CAP has functioned, and that are also of great importance in their own right: Head Start,[15] legal services, and family planning.

HEAD START

Project Head Start, developed in early 1965, was first operated during the summer of that year, when over half a million four- and five-year-old children were given six or eight weeks of special services. Few would argue that disadvantaged children from disadvantaged areas enter public school poorly equipped to compete with other children of the same age, and that a consequence of this initial inequality of opportunity is that such children will tend to fall behind. The idea behind Head Start was to give these children a better chance—in the shape of a "head start"—before their formal schooling began. The form of the program was consonant with the general principles of community action. In addition to schooling in small classes, it provided medical and dental care, social and nutritional services, and, perhaps most important, was required by statute to "provide for direct participation of the parents of such children in the development, conduct, and overall program direction at the local level."[16] Thus within a given community there would be involvement on the part of parents, doctors, nurses, teachers, and volunteers—in a very real sense the whole community would be mobilized for the effort.

Studies of the program have indicated that there is a tendency for the benefits of Head Start to attenuate over time. This is not altogether surprising, as the children, once given their preschool aid, continue to live in the same disadvantaged neighborhoods. For this reason OEO proposed a follow-through program, to be delegated to the Office of Education of the Department of Health,

[15] Head Start was transferred in 1969 to the Department of Health, Education, and Welfare, but it still functions very much as described here. As CAP's largest program for a number of years, it merits examination in this chapter.

[16] Economic Opportunity Amendments of 1967, 81 Stat. 698.

Education, and Welfare, under which special services of the type provided by Head Start would be given to Head Start pupils for their first few years of formal education. Such a program, officially called Follow Through, was required in the 1967 amendments. It was hoped that it would help to solidify and retain the initial gains made under the preschool program.

Head Start became by far the largest of the special emphasis programs of community action before being transferred to HEW. While it was originally designed exclusively as a summer program, a full-year program was soon developed. This was a good deal more expensive, and fewer children could be accommodated than in the summer program. The summer program was gradually reduced in size (from 560,000 children in fiscal 1965 to 473,000 in 1968) as the full-year program expanded from 160,000 children in fiscal 1966 to 218,000 in 1968. In fiscal 1969 both expenditures and enrollment dropped—$277 million was spent on the summer program which served 420,000 children in 1,100 communities, and on the full-year program which served 173,000 children in 800 communities. Follow Through operated in 40 communities and served 4,000 children during the 1967–68 academic year and in 80 communities with 12,000 children during 1968–69, under a $15 million grant.[17] In many areas, particularly during the summer, Head Start is the only real evidence that a war on poverty is in progress.

LEGAL SERVICES

Legal services is much more modest in scope than Head Start ($43 million as compared with $277 million in fiscal 1969) but it is still a significant endeavor. For the poor, in the words of former Justice Abe Fortas, "the law has always been the hostile policeman on the beat, the landlord who has come to serve an eviction notice, the installment seller who has come to repossess . . ." Furthermore, the poor "hate lawyers, and they have reason to, because, in their experience, the lawyer has been the agent, the tool of the oppressor."[18] The poor have traditionally regarded the law as something to be used against them, and access to their own lawyers has gener-

---

[17] Sar A. Levitan, *The Great Society's Poor Law: A New Approach to Poverty* (Johns Hopkins Press, 1969), pp. 139, 163.
[18] U.S. Office of Economic Opportunity, *The Poor Seek Justice* (1967), p. 25.

ally been unavailable to them. In consequence, the poor have been pushed around, they have been made subject to arbitrary and capricious welfare rules, public housing regulations, police action, and the like.

The legal services program is designed to help change this. During fiscal year 1968 it operated 850 law offices staffed by 1,800 lawyers in low-income neighborhoods, either in the community action agency or the neighborhood center or in conjunction with them, and 475,000 poor people received some form of legal assistance. Some of this assistance was felt by one or two poor people only, as in a domestic relations problem, but other cases—the successful challenge to an eviction regulation, for example—have had far-reaching ramifications. Lawyers in the program seek test cases that have side consequences and that will eliminate some of the arbitrariness that has grown up in administrative dealings with the poor. They do not hesitate to bring suit against a city, or a public health office, or the CAA or OEO itself if the interests of a poor client require it.

Of 327,000 people who sought help in fiscal year 1967, 11 percent were turned away because they did not really need legal advice, they were ineligible under the indigency standard, or their problems involved a case that a private attorney would take on a contingent-fee basis. Of the rest, 35 percent involved family problems of one sort or another, 26 percent had to do with landlord-tenant and consumer problems, and 32 percent involved juvenile delinquency school cases and misdemeanors. In 25 percent of the cases an appearance in court was required.

The 1967 amendments required that "no funds or personnel made available" for the legal services program "shall be utilized for the defense of any person indicted . . . for the commission of a crime, except in extraordinary circumstances. . . ."[19] This will tend to weaken one of the positive impacts that the legal services program might have had in poor communities—getting the full confidence of the poor. It makes even more important the educational part of the program, which is designed to teach the indigent the meaning and purposes of the law. In this connection, local groups such as Parent-Teacher Associations, VISTA, and legal services lawyers work together to provide the poor with instruction

[19] 81 Stat. 699.

and materials in legal education. Nearly two million had received such instruction by the end of June 1967.

FAMILY PLANNING

We turn briefly now to a program that was not strictly a special emphasis program until 1969. It is a program that is important in its own right and is also an interesting example of the interaction between analysis and policy making. It is called "Family Planning," and is concerned with the provision of advice and devices to facilitate family planning for the poor. If this is not the most cost-effective antipoverty measure, it must surely be second-best. An examination of the relation between poverty and family size reveals that in 1966 the poverty incidence among families with one child was 9 percent; as family size increased so did the incidence, reaching 42 percent for families with six or more children.[20] In part, but only in part, this is accounted for by the rising poverty line as the number of children increases. Another way to look at this is to observe that, while the average age of wives at the birth of the first child is twenty-one where family income is under $3,000, it is twenty-four where income is $10,000 or more.

Another fact of great importance is that surveys show that poor women want no more children than nonpoor women have, and perhaps fewer.[21] In fact they have more. As one might expect, poor women use birth control methods less frequently, less regularly, and beginning at a later date than do the nonpoor, because of ignorance or the lack of availability of information or services.

What would happen if poor families had the number of children they wanted, rather than the number they actually have? Surveys[22] indicate that there are about 450,000 children born each year who are unwanted at the time of conception. If these children were not born, there would be 450,000 fewer poor each year, plus all those who would move across the poverty line by virtue of being in smaller families.

[20] Mollie Orshansky, "The Shape of Poverty in 1966," *Social Security Bulletin*, Vol. 31 (March 1968), p. 7.
[21] Levitan, *The Great Society's Poor Law*, p. 207.
[22] The most recent are reported in the *New York Times*, Oct. 25, 1969.

There is no compulsion of any sort in the family planning proposal. Any family that wanted ten children would have them (and probably twelve!), but on the average poor families would have fewer children. In effect the poor would be given the same option now open to the rest of the population, an option they would be free to use or not as they saw fit. Furthermore, the cost of supplying advice and devices is estimated at a maximum of $20 per woman per year. With about five million poor women of child-bearing age, the cost would run to perhaps $100 million if they all took advantage of it, although not all of them would.[23]

Unmarried women present a more difficult problem. Unfortunately, illegitimacy among the poor, as indeed among the non-poor, is a real problem. Nothing seems to lock a young woman into poverty as surely as having a child out of wedlock, particularly if she is in her teens. The cause of the war against poverty would be well served by helping these unmarried women not to have children, but the argument for providing them with contraceptive information and devices is more subject to attack on moral grounds than in the case of married women.

All these facts were known or became known early in the war on poverty. Family planning was, from the start, a proper component in any community action application, and this was made clear. At the same time the agency did not urge communities to include family planning in their applications, preferring to play the passive role. The agency felt it could not afford to get too far ahead of the Congress on what is still a touchy issue in many quarters, and it felt that it was being rather bold in making family planning available for those communities that asked for it. Given its apparent cost-effectiveness, there were those, including the author, who pressed for having a more positive role played by the national office. However, those making the decision, notably the director himself, felt that this might jeopardize the progress being made.

The progress was modest. In the first fiscal year five communities established family planning programs. The number gradually

[23] Planned Parenthood-World Population, "Family Planning and Infant Mortality: An Analysis of Priorities" (Planned Parenthood-World Population, 1967; processed), pp. 8, 16.

increased thereafter but is still not large. For example, Planned Parenthood-World Population regards fifty-six counties of the United States as critical because they have the greatest number of "excess" infant deaths (many of them are no doubt poverty counties), and in these OEO has only 19 family planning projects operating.[24] In fiscal year 1968 the total number of OEO-funded family planning projects was only 159, at a cost of some $9 million.

The agency also imposed fairly strict guidelines. Devices would be supplied only to married women living with their husbands; no more than $12 per year could be spent on one woman (later raised to $20); no woman could receive more than one year of services (later revoked). Disagreements covering the "married living with husband" requirement were finally resolved by an amendment to the statute in 1966 stating that OEO should not determine the conditions of family planning services, thus putting the married-unmarried issue up to the local communities.

Here was a case where analysis argued strongly for an all-out campaign, even as early as 1965, but policy was slow to follow. While the 1967 amendments to the Economic Opportunity Act recognized family planning as a troublesome problem and gave the program special emphasis status, the "special" continued to be accented at the expense of the "emphasis." The go-slow policy on the program was reversed in 1969, when President Nixon made the problem the subject of a presidential message; among other things he called for a stepping up of OEO and HEW programs in the area.[25] The need for family planning has at last achieved national recognition.

Allocation of Funds to CAAs

In early 1969 there were more than one thousand community action agencies throughout the United States. They existed in all fifty states and all fifty metropolitan areas where the greatest num-

---

[24] "Family Planning and Infant Mortality," pp. 1–3. Excess infant deaths are defined as those over 18.3 per 1,000 live births.

[25] "Problems of Population Growth," *Weekly Compilation of Presidential Documents,* Vol. 5 (July 21, 1969), pp. 1000–08.

ber of poor live. No one knows how many of the poor are being reached by these CAAs, but the number is probably less than the data might indicate, and surely no more than a small fraction of the poor. Since many CAAs are either in the program development stage or are single-component affairs, many areas are really not covered by a comprehensive CAA.

One way to obtain some approximate notion of what community action must mean is to assume that the 500 comprehensive CAAs are in areas containing half the poor, or 12 million poor people. If it is assumed further that two-thirds of the $710 million of federal funds for fiscal 1969 went to these 500 CAAs, this would mean on the average an expenditure of about $40 per poor person in those areas. To be sure, most CAAs are able to mobilize some other funds, but even so the sum will remain small. It is bound to be the case that (at current levels of funding) many poor people are not touched at all.

This raises a question about the allocation of funds: If the limitation of funds is severe, should there be fewer CAAs with more resources available to each? The statute requires an "equitable" distribution of community action funds among states and the criteria of equity are spelled out. Basically, the available funds are to be given to the states in relative amounts determined by the number of public assistance recipients, the rate of unemployment, and the number of children in low-income families as compared with the national average. Within states there is to be equity between rural and urban areas, to be determined in light of the above criteria plus several additional ones—numbers of school dropouts, draft rejectees, and adults with less than an eighth-grade education. Under the 1967 amendments, the director is allowed to reserve 20 percent of the funds for allotment "in accordance with such criteria and procedures as he may prescribe."[26] This, and the fact that the director is free to weight the statutory criteria as he sees fit, gives to OEO a considerable freedom to allocate its resources, scarce as they may be.

A case has been made that, even if they were taken literally, these criteria could be used to direct funds to those areas where poverty was most concentrated. It was argued, for example, when

[26] 81 Stat. 702.

allocation guidelines were being evolved, that CAP funds should go only to those rural areas containing counties which were in the two poorest quintiles, and in urban areas only to those census tracts which were in the poorest quartile of all tracts. This would have put the funds in areas where the poor were concentrated, would have made many areas simply ineligible, at least so long as funds were limited, and would have resulted in far more resources per poor person than in those areas where funds did go.

Instead, funds were spread as applications came in, and the result was a thin coverage of many places (but very few congressional districts were left out), with questionable impact. In New York City, for example, the welfare budget is now over a billion dollars annually,[27] whereas CAP funds, even though New York City draws more than its "fair share," amount to about $50 million annually. At this level it is difficult to discern any impact; this has been one of the factors plaguing the war on poverty—almost everywhere the resources are too small to show impact. The idea of concentrating resources in a large way in a few experimental instances ought to receive more serious consideration. Only in this way will it be possible to reach some judgment on whether community action, properly funded and concentrated, will accomplish what it is supposed to.

Community action agencies are designed to do much more than administer the special emphasis programs. In fact and, in light of congressional earmarking, somewhat ambiguously, the special emphasis programs are only to be employed where "the Director determines that the objectives sought could not be effectively achieved through the use of authorities under section 221," the general provisions for financial assistance to CAAs. It is in these general provisions that the scope of community action can be seen, for they provide federal grants to help in local planning and coordination of programs which impinge on almost every aspect of American poverty. More may be written about the special emphasis programs, because more is available about them and they are nationwide in impact; yet it is local initiative that is the crux of

[27] *Income Maintenance Programs*, Vol. 2: *Appendix Materials*, Hearings before the Subcommittee on Fiscal Policy of the Joint Economic Committee, 90 Cong. 2 sess. (1968), p. 500.

CAP, and to local initiative we now turn, dealing with the role of community action in three major areas of deficiency which are first concerns of other agencies. These are health, education, and housing, all of great importance to the poor—the lack of any or all of them is highly correlated with poverty. It is part of the role of the CAA to bring to the relevant agencies its specialized local knowledge of these problems in a given geographic area.

HEALTH

As with so many unpleasant aspects of life, ill health affects the poor more than the nonpoor. The poor suffer more from chronic diseases, miss work more often because of sickness, utilize doctors, dentists, and hospitals less often, but when they do use them they are likelier to be more seriously ill and require more intensive use of them.

It is an anomaly that expenditures per capita by and on behalf of the poor for medical care are not very different from those for the population as a whole. Part of this is government money, and the proportion will increase as Medicare and Medicaid become more important. But if amounts per capita are not unduly low, somehow the quality of the medical care for the poor has been low.[28] Frequently the facilities are difficult to reach (for example, there was no medical facility in Watts when the war on poverty was launched); the long hard bench with the long wait is all too common; and the service tends to be utterly impersonal when it is finally delivered. All these drawbacks tend to make the poor reluctant to use the facilities, and thus illness is more severe when they finally do.

OEO began experimenting early with the neighborhood health center, which it regarded as the answer to the problem. Located in the community action agency, or at least in the poverty area, the NHC provides comprehensive medical and dental care for the poor. It pulls together services provided by the Children's Bureau, the Public Health Service, and other agencies, and fills any gaps that exist. In one of the early and successful centers (that in Den-

[28] See *Economic Report of the President, February 1968,* pp. 157–61.

ver) OEO funds amounted to less than half of the total.[29] For the first time the poor had a center to which the whole family could go, where all services were available, and which was easily accessible. In 1966 the Congress added a comprehensive health services program among its amendments to the Economic Opportunity Act, and this was included among the special emphasis programs in the 1967 amendments. Health centers are now planned in conjunction with the Department of Health, Education, and Welfare.

These centers are still quite experimental. It is not clear how many people should be served, how to handle the nonpoor who want the services, how much effort to put into getting people to come in for preventive treatment, and so on. Furthermore, the centers are expensive, even when other sources of funds can be tapped. OEO spent about $50 million in fiscal 1969 on some forty grants. The centers thus far established reach something over a million people, which suggests the magnitude of the problem.

EDUCATION

In education, community action has been content to supplement the public school system through Head Start, some remedial tutorial programs, and some adult literacy facilities. This is not enough, since lack of education is so central to the poverty problem. Furthermore, it is in the poverty areas that facilities of all sorts are poorest. In them are normally found lower per capita expenditures, less experienced teaching and administrative personnel, older and less modern facilities, and less up-to-date curricula. In addition, the massive report prepared by the Office of Education in 1966[30] makes abundantly clear that the educational system is still essentially a segregated one, and that the fact of segregation is a powerful element in the inferiority of education in many poverty areas.

The government's answer to this problem thus far has been the Elementary and Secondary Education Act of 1965.[31] Title I of this

[29] Presumably, when Colorado initiates Medicaid, the OEO share will decline.

[30] James S. Coleman and others, *Equality of Educational Opportunity*, U.S. Office of Education (1966).

[31] 79 Stat. 27.

statute provides financial assistance for schools in disadvantaged areas; annual appropriations of about one billion dollars have been made. This money is spent through state education agencies in accordance with state plans submitted to the Office of Education for approval. Community action agencies have been a part of this process in that they see and approve the local school plans for the expenditure of these funds at the time the plans are submitted to the state. In this way the CAA keeps abreast of how educational expenditures for the benefit of the poor are being made.

Title I money is unfortunately unlikely to conquer the problem of education in the slums. The difficulty seems to be that it is becoming clear that the factors that can be varied with money are not very closely related to the achievement of school pupils.[32] The Coleman study strongly indicates that the factors that account most for the variation in the performances of children across the country are, in order of importance:

1. The backgrounds of the peer group. A black student from a slum background is much more likely to do well if he is in a school where a large number of the pupils are white middle-class, and is thus able to mix with young people whose values are more achievement-oriented with regard to schooling.

2. The general quality of the teaching staff, both in terms of its professional qualifications and its homogeneity with, and sympathy for, the student body.

3. Physical facilities, such as laboratories and classrooms.

The money provided under the 1965 act is most effective only with the least salient of these factors and can have little or no effect on the peer group and the home.

Meanwhile, education in the slums appears to improve little if at all. In many central cities the Negro population is growing rapidly, and the school population becomes ever more heavily Negro

---

[32] This conclusion is substantially that of Stephen K. Bailey and Edith K. Mosher in their recent analysis of the Elementary and Secondary Education Act of 1965, *ESEA: the Office of Education Administers a Law* (Syracuse University Press, 1968). In their conclusion they state: "Even if more rational and aggressive Federal policies were developed to change the ecology of learning for low status children, there is mounting evidence that American educators do not know how to teach the poor" (p. 222). If indeed this is the case, it is clear that the short-run impact can be expected to be low, as these authors' investigations have revealed it to be.

as white families escape to suburbs or private schools. While smaller classes, better facilities, and other things money buys must help somewhat, the problem is far from solution. What is needed is some sort of breakthrough which can go to the root of the trouble. It may be that the notion of the educational park will develop into such a breakthrough.[33]

HOUSING

Improved housing is always high on the list of what the poor want, and the coincidence between poor housing and poverty is great. If the model cities program[34] should ever get off the ground, CAAs could have a major role to play in helping to plan neighborhood development for poverty areas, but the problem now is that private enterprise is simply unable to build housing that can be provided at prices the poor are able to pay. For example, the least poor family of four ought to pay about $50 per month for housing; housing for this figure cannot be built, and existing housing of decent quality is hardly available at this price either. As a consequence, the poor are forced to rent (or rarely, buy) housing that is old and undesirable. Though the housing situation has been improving over time, about four million poor families still live in housing that is unsafe, overcrowded, or lacks adequate plumbing facilities.[35] And while housing for the poor improves, it does so less rapidly than for the nonpoor so that the gap continues to grow.

Up to now, very little has been done about housing for the poor. The largest program has been and still is public housing—

[33] The educational park is a large comprehensive school located between ghetto and suburban areas, to which all sorts of children would come by bus. It would permit integration in whatever proportion desired, eliminate the present tendency of the best teachers to seek the easiest school situations, and be large enough to permit economies that come from specialization.

[34] The model cities program, adopted by Congress in 1966 as the demonstration cities program (80 Stat. 1255), is designed to demonstrate how city governments and neighborhood residents planning jointly can overcome their social and economic problems through the concerted use of federal, state, local, and private funds. As of early 1969, 150 communities had been selected for the programs. *The Budget of the United States Government, Fiscal Year 1970*, p. 126.

[35] See U.S. Office of Economic Opportunity, *Community Action and Urban Housing* (1967), p. 9.

subsidized housing made available to low-income families. As of 1969 there were only some 700,000 public housing units, although the program began in 1937; in recent years the number of units constructed has been about 30,000 annually, although the tempo increased somewhat in the late 1960s.[36] Not only is this number so small as to make no noticeable impression on the problem, but these public housing units have never been popular with the poor, who regard the rules of occupancy as unreasonable and who feel that they are little more than a new form of segregated living. In many cities the architecture has been lacking in imagination.

The government is trying to nibble away at the housing problem. Section 221(d)(3) of the National Housing Act as amended by the Housing Act of 1961 provides low-interest loans for the construction of housing, but other costs force this into the category of middle-income housing.[37] The rent-supplement plan enacted in 1965, whereby poor people would receive rent subsidies, has real promise, since it may enable the Negro poor to get away from segregated housing; but Congress has been niggardly in appropriating funds for it. The irony of this is that the income tax laws are rigged to give very substantial subsidies to middle-income and upper-income groups who customarily own their own homes. Deductions for interest payments and local taxes are estimated to have amounted to $2.9 billion for the richest 20 percent of the population in 1966.[38]

The decent housing now available for the poor is grossly inadequate and in the normal course of events it is unlikely that the situation will improve. What is needed is a massive public effort. The National Commission on Urban Problems has recom-

[36] *A Decent Home*, Report of the President's Committee on Urban Housing, Edgar F. Kaiser, Chairman (1969), pp. 60–61.

[37] 48 Stat. 1246; 75 Stat. 150. See also Frank S. Kristof, *Urban Housing Needs Through the 1980's: An Analysis and Projection*, Prepared for the Consideration of the National Commission on Urban Problems, Paul H. Douglas, Chairman (1968), pp. 52–53. For a discussion of housing problems in poverty areas, see another report prepared for the commission by Allen D. Manvel, *Housing Conditions in Urban Poverty Areas* (1968). For the final recommendations, see *Building the American City*, Report of the National Commission on Urban Problems to the Congress and to the President of the United States, H. Doc. 91–34, 91 Cong. 1 sess. (1968).

[38] Henry J. Aaron, "Income Taxes and Housing," to appear in a forthcoming issue of the *American Economic Review*.

mended that 500,000 houses a year be built for those below or just above the official poverty level (exclusive of the elderly).[39]

What is the role of community action in dealing with the problem of housing for the poor? In the words of OEO, it is largely to "push, prod, and persuade . . . [the relevant] agencies to tailor their programs to meet, in an effective way, the housing problems of poor people."[40] It is more than that. Within the general scheme of community action, poor people wishing to make complaints either to landlords or to welfare agencies can come to the neighborhood center and receive legal advice and perhaps some political support. Furthermore, just as the CAA can push the housing agencies, so can it push the poor people to become informed about the kind of aid they are eligible for. The main problem is that adequate housing does not exist, but community action has a role in working toward the creation of housing in the manner best suited to the needs of the individual community.

There is one distinctive feature of housing services which acts to compound the problem. The supply of these services is what economists call highly inelastic. That is, if somehow the income deficiency of the poor could be remedied, they would not thereby be able to buy the housing services they wanted. The response of the quantity of housing available to new demand is very slow; for a considerable period the change in the demand-supply situation would simply push up the sale and rental price of housing, which would be of little help to the poor. For this reason the housing problem, more than most others, needs attention on both the supply and the demand side.

We conclude this chapter as we began it. Community action is a novel and flexible instrument, its main purpose being to deal with all of the facets of poverty at once. To do this it performs the functions of delivering services, coordinating programs, mobilizing local resources, and above all enabling the poor to participate in solving their own problems. While it is not and cannot be a fo-

[39] This would not eliminate all substandard housing, but it would give to the poor a much better opportunity to escape from it. *Building the American City*, p. 180.

[40] U.S. Office of Economic Opportunity, *Community Action and Urban Housing*, pp. 15–16.

menter of social revolution, it can and often does take the position of the "establishment radical." The concept of local initiative, so central to the original idea, is in some jeopardy, but it remains important, although local initiative now rests more with the local governments than it once did. The total impact of community action has been less than the controversy it has stirred up might lead one to think, but its promise is as easily visible as its need for greater funding. The Nixon administration's decision to retain community action for at least another two years was first announced in the President's message to Congress on February 19, 1969; it was amplified in a presidential message of August 11, 1969 and in a speech by OEO Director Donald Rumsfeld on October 13, 1969.[41] Its near-term future is thus apparently assured, and its evolution will be interesting to watch. New developments, like model cities, community development corporations, and other community betterment efforts that can be expected, will, or at least should, find community action agencies a valuable ally in both planning and implementation. As these developments appear, the role of "spokesman for the poor" will receive a continuing test.

[41] "The Nation's Antipoverty Programs" and "Office of Economic Opportunity," in *Weekly Compilation of Presidential Documents*, Vol. 5 (1969), pp. 282–87, 1132–36; Donald Rumsfeld, address before the National Association for Community Development, Silver Spring, Md.

CHAPTER V

Manpower and Employment Policy

We turn from specific programs administered by the Office of Economic Opportunity to examine the total poverty problem and consider what kinds of solutions can be developed. Our interest here is in the whole federal government, not simply the Office of Economic Opportunity. We shall look at the poverty question through the eyes of the President's chief of staff, not the director of OEO. It will be recalled that he has two hats.

We have already made the point that manpower problems are central to the poverty problem. OEO employs some poor people, trains a few, educates a few more, and finds jobs for some. But most manpower money is spent by other agencies—the Manpower Administration in the Labor Department, the Bureau of Adult Vocational and Technical Education in the Office of Education, and others. Job availability stems largely from the state of the economy, which is the primary concern of the Council of Economic Advisers, the Treasury, and the Bureau of the Budget. All of these things are directly relevant to poverty, perhaps more so than some of the measures that fall bureaucratically under OEO.

As a preliminary to the discussion, let us define a few terms. The employed are the sum of those engaged in either part-time or full-time remunerative activity. The unemployed are all those not employed but actively seeking work. The labor force consists of the employed plus the unemployed. The labor force participation rate is the percentage of the total population that is in the labor force. The unemployment rate is the percentage of the labor force that is unemployed. The term "employable" refers to those who are not disqualified from work by such causes as age, illness, disability, or family situation (mothers with children under age eighteen), as opposed to the term "labor force," which refers only to those who are working or seeking work. Unemployables are precluded from work by age, illness, disability, and so on.

It is incorrect to assume an identity between the poor and the unemployed. Indeed, most of the poor are not unemployed, and most of the unemployed are not poor. Nonetheless, for the poor the state of the labor market is critical. A healthy economy with a high level of employment and a good growth rate will not eliminate poverty, but without these things nothing else will. The impact of a healthy economy "not only will eliminate that poverty which is solely due to unemployment, but, by setting off market processes which tend to raise low wages faster than high wages, it will in time greatly diminish the poverty due to low incomes from jobs. In addition, by drawing additional workers into the labor force, tight full employment will increase the number of families with more than one worker."[1] We shall presently examine a number of the implications of this statement.

The importance of employment is historically demonstrable as well. Weisbrod has divided the years from 1948 to 1963 into years of strong economic expansion, weak expansion, and no expansion. He found that in the years of strong expansion the number of poor families on the average declined by 667,000 per year; in those of weak expansion, by 425,000 families; and in the no expansion years, the number of poor families *rose* by 400,000 per year on the average. Weisbrod considers this as strong evidence that the effect of expansion is a "powerful" one.[2] Other evidence could be adduced if necessary; it seems incontrovertible that the best friend a poverty warrior has is that set of policies that will assure a strong demand for labor.

[1] Hyman P. Minsky, "The Role of Employment Policy," in Margaret S. Gordon (ed.), *Poverty in America* (Chandler, 1965), p. 177.

[2] Burton A. Weisbrod (ed.), *The Economics of Poverty: An American Paradox* (Prentice-Hall, 1965), pp. 15–16. He uses a simple $3,000 family-income definition of poverty.

Effect of Economic Conditions

It is perhaps implicit in some of these data that the impact on the poor of changes in the state of the economy is greater than it is on the nonpoor. The point should be made explicit since it is an important one. It does seem to be the case that the poor stand at the end of the hiring line and that they are the first to be laid off as well. In the case of Negroes, who are so overrepresented among the poor, "a fall in the level of employment has almost twice as much effect on Negro as on white incomes. . . . Negro incomes fall almost twice as fast as white. . . . In expansions the relations are reversed and Negroes make larger relative income gains."[3] For teen-agers and other disadvantaged groups in the labor market the story is similar.[4]

It would seem that the poor generally participate in the labor market much less than the nonpoor. In 1966, for example, under the unrevised definition of poverty, of all nonpoor household heads (including one-person households) 96.7 percent of those under sixty-five worked at some time during the year and 88.3 percent worked full time for over thirty-nine weeks. For those in poverty, however, the two percentages were 73.0 and 42.1.[5] Partly this is because so many more poor households are headed by women, but even for males the difference is significant (97.8 and 90.4 as against 83.8 and 55.0). These data highlight the fact that the labor market does less for the poor than for the nonpoor. This is true partly because the poor participate less and are less able to participate in

[3] Lester C. Thurow, "The Role of Manpower Policy in Achieving Aggregate Goals," in Robert A. Gordon (ed.), *Toward a Manpower Policy* (Wiley, 1967), p. 88. This relationship is examined in more detail in Thurow, *Poverty and Discrimination* (Brookings Institution, 1969), Chap. 3.

[4] Arthur M. Okun, "The Role of Aggregate Demand in Alleviating Unemployment," and William G. Bowen, "Unemployment in the United States: Quantitative Dimensions," in William G. Bowen and Frederick H. Harbison (eds.), *Unemployment in a Prosperous Economy:* A Report of The Princeton Manpower Symposium, May 13–14, 1965 (Industrial Relations Section, Princeton University, 1965), pp. 67–81, 15–44.

[5] U.S. Office of Economic Opportunity, "Dimensions of Poverty in 1964–1965–1966" (Dec. 10, 1968; processed), Tables 4B, 4C.

the labor market, and partly because they carry a higher incidence of unemployment.

Since by definition the need for income is more acute for the poor than for the nonpoor, it is ironic that more of the poor are neither employed nor unemployed, but are simply not in the labor market. This is largely a function of the state of the economy. Many of the poor, and particularly the minority groups among them, stay in the labor market looking for work for a while, and then become discouraged and withdraw—they no longer seek employment and therefore are no longer counted as being in the labor market. If the job situation should become more favorable, however, they would reenter the market. This behavior is particularly true of nonwhite secondary workers. Nonwhite married women with husbands in the home join the job market in significant numbers when jobs become plentiful. This indicates, among other things, that the number of unemployed poor does not accurately reflect the number who would benefit from an improvement in the employment situation.

This tendency of poor people to come into the labor market as jobs become easier to get and to exit from it as the unemployment rate rises has been called the "discouraged worker" hypothesis. An opposite hypothesis, known as the "additional worker" hypothesis, argues that as unemployment rates rise, family income will fall and this will force families to send extra members out in search of work to try to protect the family income. These additional workers would presumably leave the labor market as jobs became easier and the chief breadwinner became employed once more. Whichever hypothesis fits the facts for the labor force in general, there can be little doubt that the poor behave in accordance with the discouraged worker hypothesis.[6] This is but another indication of how important appropriate aggregate demand policies are for the war against poverty.

When the poor do participate in the labor market, they do so less effectively than do the nonpoor. They tend to be unemployed more often, to receive lower wages, and to have more part-time

[6] See Joseph D. Mooney, "Urban Poverty and Labor Force Participation," *American Economic Review*, Vol. 57 (March 1967), pp. 104–19.

TABLE 5

Changes in the Number and Percentage of Poor, by Selected Characteristics, 1959–63 and 1963–67

(Numbers in millions)

Sex and family status	1959			1963						1967					
				Total		White		Nonwhite[a]		Total		White		Nonwhite[a]	
	Total	White	Non-white[a]	Number	Annual percentage change 1959–63	Number	Annual percentage change 1959–63	Number	Annual percentage change 1959–63	Number	Annual percentage change 1963–67	Number	Annual percentage change 1963–67	Number	Annual percentage change 1963–67
In families	34.6	24.4	10.1	31.5	−2.3	21.1	−3.6	10.3	0.5	22.8	−7.8	14.9	−8.3	7.9	−6.4
Male head	27.5	20.2	7.4	23.9	−3.4	17.1	−4.1	6.8	−2.1	15.9	−9.7	11.4	−9.6	4.5	−9.8
Children under 18	13.1	9.0	4.1	11.1	−4.1	7.5	−4.5	3.6	−3.2	7.2	−10.3	4.8	−10.6	2.4	−9.6
Female head	7.0	4.2	2.8	7.6	2.1	4.1	−0.6	3.6	−6.5	6.9	−2.4	3.5	−3.9	3.4	−1.4
Children under 18	4.1	2.4	1.7	4.6	2.9	2.3	−1.1	2.3	7.8	4.2	−2.2	1.9	−4.7	2.3	0.0
Unrelated	4.9	4.0	0.9	4.9	0.0	4.1	0.6	0.8	−2.9	5.0	0.5	4.1	0.0	0.9	3.0
Male	1.5	1.2	0.4	1.5	0.0	1.2	0.0	0.3	0.0	1.3	−3.5	1.0	−4.5	0.3	0.0
Female	3.4	2.9	0.5	3.5	0.7	2.9	0.0	0.5	0.0	3.7	1.4	3.1	1.7	0.5	0.0
Total	39.5	28.5	11.0	36.4	−2.0	25.2	−3.0	11.2	0.4	27.8	−6.5	19.0	−6.8	8.8	−5.9

Source: U.S. Bureau of the Census, Current Population Reports, Series P-60, No. 68, "Poverty in the United States: 1959 to 1968" (1969), p. 21; percentages are derived from information on p. 24. Figures are rounded and do not necessarily add to totals.

a. Negro and other races.

employment. In fact, it is just for these reasons that many of them are poor. Because of this, the generalization asserted earlier holds: full employment, by alleviating a situation in which there is widespread unemployment and part-time employment, is an essential condition for combating poverty. To illustrate this point and give it substance, we shall compare the magnitude and composition of changes in the poverty population over two four-year periods— 1959–63 and 1963–67.

The four years between 1959 and 1963 were years of slow economic growth. The unemployment rate for all workers over the period averaged 5.8 percent; for whites it was 5.2 percent and for nonwhites 11.1 percent. The number of persons in poverty declined during this period by 3.1 million (an annual change of −2.0 percent); the net decline occurred entirely in the category of households headed by males. While the number of children in poverty in households headed by a nonwhite male declined, the number in households headed by nonwhite females rose substantially. (See Table 5.) The total number of nonwhites in poverty rose slightly.[7]

The period from 1963 to 1967 was one of considerably more rapid growth, which toward its end approached full employment. The unemployment rates over this period were 4.3 percent for the economy as a whole, 3.8 percent for whites, and 8.1 percent for nonwhites. The difference in the magnitudes, although not the composition, of exits from poverty is striking. There was a net decline of 8.6 million persons in poverty during the period (an annual change of −6.5 percent). Only 1.1 million of these, however, were members of households headed by women; 2.4 million were nonwhites (an annual change of −5.9 percent).

Even more striking is the change from 1966 to 1967.[8] Here the unemployment rate for the population as a whole in 1967 was 3.8

---

[7] The unemployment rates in this and the following paragraph are from *Economic Report of the President, January 1969*, p. 255.

[8] The calculations are based on data from Mollie Orshansky, "The Shape of Poverty in 1966," *Social Security Bulletin*, Vol. 31 (March 1968). They are based on the old definition because, according to the Census Bureau, "due to errors affecting the income data for 1967, poverty data [revised series] for that year are not strictly comparable with those shown for 1966 and 1968." U.S. Bureau of the Census, *Current Population Reports*, Series P-60, No. 68, "Poverty in the United States: 1959 to 1968" (1969), p. 16.

percent (3.4 percent for whites and 7.4 percent for nonwhites). In this one year the number of poor people declined by 3.8 million (just 1.1 million less than in the previous three years). The percentage change was − 12.8, and a total of one million of the 3.8 were nonwhites (− 10.8 percent annual change). Again, however, all but 500,000 of the poverty exits were accounted for by members of households headed by men.

Two points emerge from this experience. A heated-up economy is necessary, and quite effective, in reducing the extent of poverty among those connected with or easily brought into labor markets. It has almost no effect, on the other hand, for those not so connected. As jobs become more plentiful and manpower becomes more scarce, it becomes profitable and necessary for employers to hire and train the disadvantaged; thus healthy males and their dependents will be beneficially affected. Others, however, such as women with large numbers of children, the aged, and the disabled, are not connected to labor markets, and economic growth has little or no effect on them. The number of children in poverty in households headed by women has risen slightly since 1959. Neither the fastest growing of economies nor the best of all possible manpower policies will help these people. Policies to meet their needs will be discussed in the next chapter.

As effective as economic growth is in improving the economic well-being of persons connected (potentially or actually) to labor markets, it is considerably less effective among poor people in general than among the nonpoor. If, under the unrevised definition of poverty, all healthy poor persons between the ages of fourteen and sixty-five had participated in labor markets in 1966 at the same percentage rates as the healthy nonpoor, over 1.8 million additional persons would have been employed, and over 3 million more would have been employed full-time for forty weeks or more. (See Table 6.)

Clearly, the poor participate less than do the nonpoor. Part of the difference may be explained by unmeasured disability and unsuitability for work. Part of it is probably explained by discrimination on the hiring line. But part ought also to be attributed to the inability of the poverty population to adapt to the labor market. Perhaps lack of training, inability to move where the jobs are, or even lack of basic literacy may prevent many poor people from getting into the labor market—especially, it would seem, with regard to full-time, long-term jobs.

Of the 1.7 million employable persons who could potentially be moved into the labor force, about one-half in 1966 were males.[9] Of the 1.5 million who could be moved into full-time work, 1.1 million were males. Among these would probably be found a disproportionate number of alcoholics, drug addicts, and others who are

TABLE 6

*Working Status of Poor, 1966, Actual and at
Same Rates as Nonpoor*[a]

(*In thousands*)

			Employed			
Sex	Total aged 16–64	Civilian labor force	Total	Full-time (forty weeks or more)	Part-time and/or part-year	Unemployed all year
			Actual			
Total	13,944	8,052	7,859	2,904	4,954	193
Male	5,567	4,161	4,099	1,950	2,148	62
Female	8,377	3,891	3,760	954	2,806	131
			At same rates as nonpoor			
Total	13,944	9,765	9,722	6,250	3,472	43
Male	5,567	5,049	5,039	3,951	1,088	10
Female	8,377	4,716	4,683	2,299	2,384	33

Source: Calculations based on U.S. Office of Economic Opportunity, "Dimensions of Poverty in 1964–1965–1966" (Dec. 10, 1968; processed), Tables 4B and 4C. Figures are rounded and do not necessarily add to totals.

a. Data under the revised definition of poverty were not available in this form; thus these data are based on the unrevised definition.

psychologically unsuitable for regular work. It is doubtful whether any ordinary manpower program would be of use to these people. Of the 1.2 million females who could be moved either into the labor force or into full-time work, many were family heads with their own children. When considering a manpower policy in relation to such women, it is necessary to decide whether it is socially advantageous to ask them to leave their homes and children to enter the labor market. Even though working women have

[9] The data in this and the following paragraph are based on the unrevised definition of poverty.

this handicap, it seems reasonable that women of poor families should participate in the labor force at the same rate as nonpoor women. For practically all of the 3.2 million total, then, a policy of training and assistance in job placement would be important.

Another way in which a growing aggregate demand is important is in creating opportunities for the clients of the training and placement programs. Even with low unemployment rates and equal labor force participation of poor and nonpoor, millions of new opportunities will have to be created to absorb the 3.2 million. Manpower programs which train and place workers will be important in this phase, but will be ineffective in reducing poverty unless a high level of aggregate demand creates new opportunities. Otherwise, even if the client of a manpower program succeeds in finding a job, some other near-poor worker will probably be ousted from a job. Manpower programs without an expanding economy tend simply to shuffle the available jobs among the poor and near-poor.

If high employment is so critical, why does the government not simply push down the unemployment rate with the appropriate fiscal and monetary policies? The answer is that as the unemployment rate declines the danger of inflation increases, and difficult choices become necessary. Economists have been studying this relation for some time, and it is still not clear just what it is, at least numerically. It is known that at some point, as unemployment falls, the general level of prices will begin to rise as bottlenecks develop here and there through the economy. From 1960 to 1965, for example, the price level was reasonably stable, rising a little over a point a year. At the same time unemployment was fairly substantial, in excess of 5 percent; but toward the end of the period it fell, to 4.5 percent in 1965, and then in 1966 to below 4 percent. The consumer price index began to rise more rapidly, increasing from 111.0 in January 1966 to 114.7 in December.[10] This experience convinced many that an unemployment rate of 3.8 percent (the 1966 average) carried with it too much inflation, and anti-inflation measures were adopted which temporarily assured that the unemployment rate would not go lower.

[10] *Economic Report of the President, February 1968*, p. 261.

Unemployment and Price Changes

To have to conclude that unemployment rates under 4 percent necessarily imply intolerable levels of inflation could be very unfortunate from the point of view of the war on poverty, since, as has been shown, the poor suffer seriously from lack of employment opportunities. The conclusion is particularly unfortunate because the relation between price changes and unemployment is not well understood. In this section the thinking that has been done on the subject will be examined, with the object of discovering some policy possibilities that will aid the poor.

The pioneering work in this field was done by A. W. Phillips.[11] He hypothesized that as the demand for labor becomes tight, bottlenecks develop and employers bid up the price of labor in an effort to attract workers. When demand falls, however, laborers are reluctant to offer their services at less than the going wage, and therefore wages fall only slowly, and only after high levels of unemployment develop. This asymmetric action of wage rates and unemployment suggests that the relationship between them is nonlinear. Phillips further suggested that when demand is growing rapidly wages might rise faster for a given level of unemployment than otherwise.

Phillips worked with British data, first for the 1861 to 1913 period. A curve relating the annual percentage change of money wages to the percentage of the labor force unemployed was fitted to the data. Since wages may change by as much as the change in labor productivity without having an inflationary impact, the level of price change indicated by a given rate of change of wage rates is found by subtracting the rate of change of labor productivity from the change of wages. Phillips found that "assuming an increase in [labor] productivity of 2 per cent. per year, it seems from the relation fitted to the data that if aggregate demand were kept at a value which would maintain a stable level of product

---

[11] "The Relation Between Unemployment and the Rate of Change of Money Wage Rates in the United Kingdom, 1861–1957," *Economica*, Vol. 25 (November 1958), pp. 283–99.

prices the associated level of unemployment would be a little under 2½ per cent."[12] The relation of the early years was compared with the observations of the interwar and postwar periods, and the fit was good, particularly recently. This relation, which is now called the Phillips curve, is very stable and at a fairly low level for Great Britain.

Two and a half percent unemployment with stable prices is quite different from recent U.S. experience. Samuelson and Solow have examined the Phillips curve relation in the United States. In the early decades of this century, they found, "wage increases equal to the productivity increase of 2 to 3 per cent per year [the amount for stable prices] (was) the normal pattern at about 3 per cent unemployment." From 1946 through the 1950s, however, the relation seemed to shift, with higher levels of unemployment associated with given changes in wages. The 2 to 3 percent per year rise in money wages which would keep prices stable seems to require "5 or 6 per cent of the labor force unemployed." The authors suggest that "in order to achieve the nonperfectionist's goal of high enough output to give us no more than 3 per cent unemployment, the price index might have to rise by as much as 4 to 5 per cent per year. That much price rise would seem to be the necessary cost of high employment and production in the years immediately ahead."[13]

Samuelson and Solow suggest several reasons for the difference in the British and American situations. First, the British labor market is more compact, which makes labor mobility easier. The unemployed in one area can respond to opportunities in other areas more easily and prices do not have to change so much in order to signal shortages. Second, the British trade union leadership is more responsible and encourages wage restraints. Third, industries have been encouraged by the British government to open plants in depressed areas, and this policy would tend to lower the level of unemployment associated with a given level of price change. Also, a deliberate policy of price restraint with a high

[12] *Ibid.*, p. 299.

[13] Paul A. Samuelson and Robert M. Solow, "Analytical Aspects of Anti-inflation Policy," in American Economic Association, *Papers and Proceedings of the Seventy-second Annual Meeting, 1959 (American Economic Review*, Vol. 50, May 1960), pp. 177–94.

level of unemployment which lasted a long time might allow unemployment to harden, with the unemployed losing their work habits and depressed areas becoming less and less desirable investment sites. If aggregate demand were then increased, even higher levels of price increases would be associated with each level of unemployment since bottlenecks would not rapidly disappear.

An argument closely related to this last one was used by Phillips in his original study. Over the business cycle, as aggregate demand rises, prices tend to increase much faster than employment, while on the downswing prices tend to level off well before employment falls. Price increases seem to be necessary to gear up the economy to a higher level of aggregate demand. This loop effect implies that the price-employment relation even of the relatively neat British data is more complex than a simple curve would suggest. The United States experienced a similar loop effect with the Korean war. The initial increase of aggregate demand in 1951 (partly inspired by some consumer scare buying) pushed the price index up 8 percent while the unemployment rate dropped to 3.3 percent. In 1952 unemployment dropped to 3.0 percent and to 2.9 percent in 1953, but prices rose by less than 3 percent over the entire two years.[14] The fact of the speedup seems to be more important than the level of aggregate demand.

The most noticeable aspect of the postwar experience in the United States is the instability of the relation. The Samuelson-Solow figures on hourly earnings versus unemployment show a great deal of variability. While the small range of unemployment experience in recent years makes the projection of a curve difficult, the relation appears to be so unstable that any level of price change may be associated with a particular level of unemployment. This instability leads to the hope that relative price stability and low unemployment are not incompatible. Perhaps some appropriate policy mix can bring stability at the 1952–53 level of 3 percent unemployment without excessive price increases.

What makes prices rise as labor becomes scarce is the development of specific labor shortages in industries and regions where

---

[14] *Economic Report of the President, January 1969*, pp. 255, 279. It is true that there were statutory price controls during this period, but it is generally recognized that these were quite ineffective and can hardly claim credit for price stability.

demand is particularly strong. Unutilized resources do not flow to the areas of shortage because resources are not completely mobile. The aircraft industry experiencing a severe shortage of skilled labor in Seattle is not helped by a surplus of unskilled unemployed labor in Appalachia. It is imperfections in the markets that bring on price increases before unemployment reaches its absolute minimum, probably somewhere around 1.5 percent.[15] Thus anything which improves mobility will permit lower unemployment rates for a given amount of price increase. Changes in the conditions of the marketplace, therefore, are very relevant to the problem, whether these changes take place because of new economic conditions or as a result of public policy measures.

Relevant too is the speed with which the unemployment rate is pushed down. Most—and ultimately all—bottlenecks are temporary. Given time, people do move to where opportunities are better, and they do take training to build up new skills. But people in the mass move slowly, and to change their location or skills takes time. It follows that if the economy heats up slowly there is a better chance for the necessary adjustments to take place without inflation.

Arthur Okun has expressed the hope that certain changes he detects may make it possible in the future to reach low unemployment levels without inflation.[16] First, he sees foreign competition as more significant in price making today than it has been in the past. This tends to keep prices down. Second, there is a better balance of demand and supply today than in the 1950s when there seemed to be excess demand in certain capital goods sectors but no general excess demand. Third, some improvement in wage and price decisions from those unions and firms with market power should result from their experience under the wage-price guidelines. And finally, manpower policies directed toward education and training have become more widespread; they are aimed at breaking the bottlenecks. There is no assurance about how significant these factors may be; perhaps, however, they argue for more experimentation in policies.

[15] There will always be some people between jobs in a dynamic economy with freedom of choice. This would keep the unemployment rate from going below about 1.5 percent.

[16] "The Role of Aggregate Demand," pp. 71–72.

The experience of the late 1960s is inconclusive. The seasonally adjusted unemployment rate first went below 4 percent in January 1966, and fluctuated between 3.3 and 4.3 during the next three years. In January 1966 the consumer price index stood at 111.0 and by the end of 1968 had risen to 123.7, which is too much but hardly catastrophic. Wholesale prices were more nearly stable, moving only from 104.6 in January 1966 to 109.8 in December 1968, three years later, by which time unemployment had reached a low of 3.3 percent.[17]

In 1969 the economy was clearly heated up and the question was what policy to follow. The 10 percent surtax, enacted in 1968,[18] no doubt helped, but there has been clamor for letting unemployment rise to ease pressure on prices. To some extent this may be necessary in the short run, but the reasoning set forth in this section argues that, in a choice between unemployment and price stability, there is a tendency to give too much weight to price stability. There should be somewhat more tolerance of rising prices in the realization that they are buying jobs for the poor who badly need the jobs, particularly since the relation is so tenuous in any case and may change after time has elapsed, as it did in 1952–53. The benefits of low unemployment are so great that more risks should be run to achieve it.[19]

Inflation and the Poor

But what about inflation's impact on the poor? Are not the poor among the worst sufferers from price rises? No one wants hyperinflation, and many people feel that a little inflation leads to more until it is running away—"a little inflation is like a little pregnancy." This is simply nonsense: the nation not only does not

[17] *Economic Report of the President, February 1968; ibid., January 1969; Economic Indicators,* prepared for the Joint Economic Committee by the Council of Economic Advisers (October 1969), pp. 10, 26, 27.

[18] Revenue and Expenditure Control Act of 1968, 82 Stat. 251.

[19] The point is that those calling the tune have seemed far more concerned with a rise in prices than with a fall in unemployment. Robert A. Gordon, *The Goal of Full Employment* (Wiley, 1967) argues persuasively that 3 percent unemployment could be achieved without undue inflation with appropriate manpower policies; pp. 181–85.

want severe inflation but it also knows how to avoid it. The question is whether people are willing to have an increase in prices somewhat larger than they experienced from 1951 to 1967 if this increases the probability of creating significantly more jobs.

There are those, even among the conservative economists, who answer this question in the affirmative. For example, Harry G. Johnson of the University of Chicago has stated:

> So far as the inflationary consequences of a higher level of demand and a lower rate of unemployment are concerned, I would argue that it would be in the social interest to endure an appreciable but not high rate of inflation—say, up to something like a 4 per cent per annum increase in the consumer price index—in order to reduce the percentage of unemployment.[20]

Perhaps more can be said about just how much moderate inflation affects the poor. It has already been urged that tight employment helps them greatly. At overall unemployment levels of 3 to 6 percent, the unemployment of the poor is probably double that of the population as a whole. One percentage point reduction in the overall rate means a reduction of at least two percentage points for the unemployed poor. Together with the increased labor force participation that goes with this improvement in the economy, the result may be an increase of as much as a half million in the employed poor, many of whom would no doubt exit from poverty and take their families with them.[21]

To turn to the cost side, and to anticipate the discussion, the conclusion is that the poor suffer from modest inflation only marginally, in any case significantly less than they benefit from the brighter employment prospects. The first thing to note is that the expenditures of the poor seem to be affected less than those of the nonpoor. The consumer price index does not adequately reflect the items purchased by poor people and is not intended to. Since 1940 the aggregate price of things poor people buy has gone up less in every period of price inflation than the consumer price index.

[20] "Unemployment and Poverty," in Leo Fishman (ed.), *Poverty amid Affluence* (Yale University Press, 1966), p. 196.

[21] This and the following paragraphs draw heavily on a paper by Robinson G. Hollister and John L. Palmer, *The Impact of Inflation on the Poor* (University of Wisconsin, Institute for Research on Poverty, 1969). The study suggests that a 1 point reduction in the overall unemployment rate would move 1.0 to 1.5 million people out of poverty. This is a one-shot result, of course.

The reasons for this are complex; they lie basically in what the poor buy. The poor buy more housing and food as a percentage of their total expenditures than the nonpoor; these about offset each other, since the price of food always increases faster than other items, and housing more slowly. The poor purchase less in the categories of clothes, transport, and medical expenses (in the future Medicare will make a great difference), and these all usually increase more than the average. This differential in favor of the poor is not great, but at least it does not make their lot more difficult.[22]

On the income side there are only spotty data, but they are fairly persuasive. It has been said that wages generally lag behind prices during inflations, but apparently this is not so; in the mild recent inflations the labor share of total income has not changed, or at least not because of the inflation.[23] Indeed, the impact on the poor is no doubt the reverse, as the lowest wages tend to gain at the expense of the average as the labor market tightens.

What of those receiving fixed incomes? There are not many truly fixed income receivers among the poor. Those receiving public assistance payments or social security receive amounts determined by public policy. If one compares these payments with price changes, he finds that they have kept pace so that the real value of the payments has not fallen. This is as true of the aged as of others. Assets held by the poor do not amount to much, and not all assets are of fixed value. Furthermore, the poor are inclined to be debtors rather than creditors, and price increases tend to make debt payment and maintenance easier.

There are no doubt some among the poor who are hurt by inflation, as there are in every group. But the evidence seems to throw real doubt on the customary view that the poor suffer more than their share in inflation. Given the clear advantage of better employment for them in general, and the failure of price increases to hurt them as much as might have been supposed, it follows that their welfare argues for pressing toward ever tighter labor markets. Three percent unemployment may be a bad policy goal because of the balance of payments, but those who would speak

[22] From 1964 to 1967 the price index for the poor rose 1 point less than the consumer price index, not allowing for the impact of Medicare.

[23] G. L. Bach and Albert Ando, "The Redistributional Effects of Inflation," *Review of Economics and Statistics*, Vol. 39 (February 1957), pp. 1–13.

against it should not invoke the welfare of the poor on their side of the argument. Such welfare requires experimentation with a heated-up economy that pushes toward 3 percent unemployment as a new interim goal.[24]

The Labor Market in the Ghetto

It has been said earlier that aggregate demand must be maintained, and the foregoing pages have indicated why. It has also been said that the maintenance of aggregate demand is not enough to do the job, and we turn now to a special aspect of the labor market for the poor that illustrates why this is so. This is a particularly unattractive corner of the labor market, which has only recently been recognized and understood, and which has generated a most serious challenge. This is the labor market in ghetto areas.

Information about the subject is based on a special study made in November 1966 of slum districts in ten areas in eight cities where poverty was severe and unemployment rates were high. This was a month when the national unemployment rate was 3.7 percent, lower than it had been for many years. The rates in the eight cities varied, some lower and some higher than the national average, but the figures were for the "labor market area," in every case including the city and some surrounding area. The special study covered only a small slum section. In these sections, the unemployment rate was found to average about 10 percent—ranging from 7 in the Roxbury area of Boston to 15.6 percent in the Hough area of Cleveland.[25]

But these figures are for the usual definition of unemployment, and the study pressed further toward what it came to call a "sub-

[24] Hollister and Palmer are in complete agreement with this goal. They conclude: ". . . if national policy makers decide that they will not explore further, but will allow unemployment to rise in hopes of stopping inflation, they will at least no longer be able to claim that they are trying to stop inflation in order to protect the poor. If any such policy is made, let it be done with the explicit recognition that, far from helping the poor, it imposes on them a very special and heavy burden." *Impact of Inflation on the Poor,* p. 52.

[25] U.S. Department of Labor, "A Sharper Look at Unemployment in U.S. Cities and Slums," A Summary Report Submitted to The President by The Secretary of Labor (no date).

employment" rate. It found that 6.9 percent of those who were listed as employed were working only part time though they wanted full-time work. It found that 21 percent of those working full time were earning less than $60 per week, the poverty figure for a person supporting three others. It found that a large number of those in the survey areas were neither working nor looking for work, so that they were not counted as unemployed. This group, called "nonparticipants," amounted to 11 percent of the men in the twenty to sixty-four age group (the figure for the nation as a whole is 7 percent). Finally, it found that between a third and a fifth of the adult males who were expected to be there were simply "unfound" in the areas. This is a common occurrence for the Census Bureau, and one not readily explainable.

The study proceeded to create a subemployment index by making a number of assumptions. It counted as subemployed those looking for work; those working part time but wanting full-time work; those heads of households under age sixty-five earning less than $60 per week at full-time jobs; those not heads of households earning less than $56 per week at full-time jobs; half the male "nonparticipants" in the twenty to sixty-four age group; and a careful estimate of the male "undercount" group, half of whom were assumed to be subemployed. For the ten areas, calculated on this basis, the average subemployment rate was 33.9 percent, ranging from a high of 47.4 percent in San Antonio to a low of 24.2 percent in Boston.

It is well to ponder these figures. They were computed at a time of enormous national prosperity, of growing labor shortages, of rising affluence. Quite obviously, this kind of failure of the labor market to function cannot be remedied by manipulating aggregate demand, though no doubt if aggregate demand were to soften, the conditions in the slums would become even worse. But other remedies are called for, remedies that are difficult and expensive, and that involve combinations of education, training, job opportunities, health services, and no doubt others.[26]

[26] That matters continued serious was indicated by a survey of six cities during the third quarter of 1968 which showed ghetto unemployment to be two and one-half times the national average. U.S. Bureau of Labor Statistics, "Employment Situation Surveyed in Slum Areas of Six Large Cities" (Feb. 20, 1969).

Proposal for Public Employment

We turn to some of the remedies proposed, particularly one worked out in the summer and fall of 1965, never adopted but still available if the resources should be forthcoming. This became known as the public employment program (PEP). In the latter part of 1965 the overall unemployment rate was about 4.5 percent, and was declining gradually toward the interim goal of 4 percent. It became clear that even if it reached this level or a bit better, there would still be a significant number of unemployed poor, since so many of them are at the end of the hiring queue (these are employable unemployed). It also became evident that public policy was not going to press the unemployment rate much below 4 percent—perhaps to 3.5 percent at best—since price increases regarded as "too severe" would begin to take place. At a point that was coming to be regarded as "full employment," significant numbers of employable poor would remain without jobs.

The arithmetic was something like the following, with most data subject to estimating errors. In 1965 there were about one million unemployed poor. To that was added some number of nonparticipants who might be expected to come into the labor market as jobs became more plentiful; the number of poor who were part of the frictionally unemployed were subtracted; the result was an estimate that from 1 to 1.5 million jobs for the poor were required. This requirement, if met, would assure the poor of a large share of new jobs as the overall unemployment rate fell to 3.5 percent. It would mean that some hiring would be done from the end of the queue. This would not entirely eliminate unemployment among the poor but it would improve their condition greatly. The proposal was that 800,000 of these jobs should be created, over a period of years and on the assumption of a 3.5 percent unemployment rate.

What would these people do? The plan was to have them work in the public sector, performing needed services, in essence making it possible to stop starving this sector and thus to improve the quality of life for all, not only for those who obtained the jobs.

OEO commissioned a study of how many such useful jobs might be created and preliminary results indicated 5.3 million, though it would be necessary to build up to this number over a period of several years. This was far more than anyone was thinking about (the final results indicated 4.3 million) and laid to rest any doubts about the ability to find or create sufficient numbers of productive jobs.[27] The job potential uncovered was as follows (details do not add to totals because of rounding):

Source of employment	Potential jobs (thousands)
Educational institutions	2,017
Medical institutions and health services	1,355
Defense	350
Public works	150
Recreation and beautification	136
Public welfare	65
Libraries	63
Police and fire	50
Institutions, dependent and delinquent children	38
Prisons	24
Other	30
Total	4,280

These would be essentially subprofessional jobs—teacher aides, nurse's aides, recreation supervisors or guards, and so on. Most were unskilled jobs that could be filled with little or no training.

The jobs were to be created by contract between the federal government, or one of its agencies such as a community action agency, and a public body (the police, the school system) or a nonprofit private body (a hospital), with the federal government supplying 90 percent of the funds, the local body the other 10 percent. The individual would then be hired by the local body just as

[27] This study was made for OEO by Arthur Greenleigh Associates. The preliminary figures were published in *Technology and the American Economy*, Report of the National Commission on Technology, Automation, and Economic Progress, Vol. 1 (February 1966), p. 36. Since then they have been widely cited, though ironically OEO never received credit for the study. The final data were published in *A Public Employment Program for the Unemployed Poor* (Greenleigh Associates, Inc., November 1965).

any other employee would be. A hospital orderly, for example, would be paid by the hospital, and need not even know he was a PEP person. The hospital would have to agree not simply to replace existing orderlies with PEP orderlies, but such maintenance-of-effort agreements are not uncommon.

Hiring would not be limited to the poor, since that would tend to stigmatize them. But hiring would be done in poverty areas, and at wages which would not attract many of the nonpoor. There would be no effort to screen out those already having jobs, or secondary workers. If the resources were adequate to hire all comers, this would mean that the government would become an employer of last resort.

These would be useful jobs, as has been emphasized, and people who held them would be expected to perform like regular employees. It is worth stressing that often they would not know they were PEP workers, and that would seem all to the good. The program would be quite flexible; as jobs in the private sector expanded, PEP would automatically have fewer takers, and conversely; or if, as might turn out to be the case, these jobs were regarded as too important to shrink in numbers, wages could be increased to retain the PEP work force intact as employment generally tightened.

One question at issue was what the wage should be, or what the range should be. The original OEO proposal was to pay the minimum wage—$1.25 at that time. Full-time employment at $1.25 per hour would amount to about $2,500 per year, below the poverty line for any family of more than two people. There was some pressure for what was termed a nonpoverty wage, perhaps $2.00 per hour. Whatever the wage, it would have a rather substantial but probably unpredictable impact on the lower end of the general wage scale, and this impact would increase as the PEP wage rose. This is not necessarily bad, since the general outlines of the impact are clear enough: low wages would in general be raised if the public employment program were at all substantial. But the impact of a wage considerably above the going wage might cause all or many of the potential PEP employers to turn down the program, as they might have to increase wages to their non-PEP employees. On balance it would seem best to begin with a modest entering wage, and raise it gradually over time.

A public employment program would not be inexpensive. At what is now called full employment, an estimated 800,000 to 1 million jobs would be needed to break the back of unemployment among the poor. Depending on the wage adopted, this would cost between $2.5 and $4 billion per year. Like all public expenditures, these would reduce the federal surplus or increase the deficit. But these expenditures would go directly to the poor, and in consequence would be particularly efficient in reducing poverty if one thinks of the impact of federal expenditures on the general level of prices. Put another way, public employment expenditures "would seem particularly effective as the fiscal policy measure to move us the last few notches toward full employment after we have nearly arrived there. . . ." The jobs would go "directly and immediately to those who need help most, and who benefit from the multiplier effect of other expenditures only indirectly and much later."[28]

Solutions Adopted

Such a public employment program would essentially "solve" the manpower problems, though there would still be those on the edge of employability who would need one form of social service or another. But it stood no chance of enactment once the Vietnam escalation began to be felt in the budget. Instead there was essentially some regrouping of manpower programs and some experimentation on a small scale with several different kinds of employment programs.

In the various amendments to the Economic Opportunity Act some new wrinkles were added. A program for community betterment and beautification was added in 1965, creating jobs for adults who were chronically unemployed and poor, with emphasis on the elderly and those in rural areas. The program, which operated as Green Thumb, was later delegated to the Department of Labor, where the concept was broadened into Operation Main-

[28] Joseph A. Kershaw, "Manpower Policy, Poverty and the State of the Economy," in Frederick H. Harbison and Joseph D. Mooney (eds.), *Critical Issues in Employment Policy*, a Report of The Princeton Manpower Symposium, May 12–13, 1966 (Industrial Relations Section, Princeton University, 1966), p. 44.

stream, "whose goal is steady work at decent pay for chronically unemployed adults of all ages."[29] The 1966 amendments added the program eventually called New Careers, to create jobs for adults in health or other public services as assistants to professional personnel. The jobs were to be created by contract between the federal government and a local agency; they were not to be dead-end jobs but were to offer some chance for advancement. Also added in 1966 was the Special Impact program, to employ the poor and chronically unemployed in improving their own poverty areas, with jobs in sanitation, building parks, rehabilitation of slum housing, and so on. There were also provisions for financial and other incentives to persuade businesses to locate in urban ghettos, and provisions for general community development. The Special Impact program was later modified and became more explicitly concerned with economic development than had been the case. In the words of OEO, "This is, in fact, a new program."[30]

There were substantial overlaps among these programs (as well as with the work experience programs) and administrators at the local level were to be excused if they really did not know whether a given job was a Special Impact job or a New Careers job. As of early 1970 the Manpower Administration was administering all of the new manpower programs, parts of the Manpower Development and Training Act (MDTA) of 1962, the manpower aspects of the Work Incentive Program set up by the 1967 amendments to the Social Security Act, what was left of work experience programs of the Economic Opportunity Act, and the Job Opportunities in the Business Sector (JOBS) program, a joint federal-private enterprise effort initiated in 1968 to employ and train the hard-core disadvantaged in the country's fifty largest cities. The National Alliance of Businessmen finds the jobs through its membership, and the Department of Labor provides the trainees; employers receive compensation when it can be shown that training the poor is costing them money.[31] These various programs expended about $1.8

[29] U.S. Office of Economic Opportunity, *The Tide of Progress* (1968), p. 77.

[30] U.S. Office of Economic Opportunity, *Narrative Summary of the Economic Opportunity Amendments of 1967* (1968), p. 3.

[31] *Manpower Report of the President,* January 1969, pp. 93, 124.

billion in 1969 and were expected to reach some 1.2 million poor persons.[32]

This consolidation no doubt helped, but it would be well to remember that the new job programs were funded at low levels, and provided therefore a small number of jobs, in view of the total requirements. The country remained very far from a comprehensive employment guarantee for everyone. Two of the most expensive manpower programs in 1968 were MDTA and Job Corps, which between them claimed 40 percent of the manpower dollar and generated no jobs at all.

The Task Remaining

The manpower programs of 1969 left a great deal to be desired. They should be central to the war on poverty, both in terms of their job creation and job training aspects. Their contribution could only be regarded as pitifully small. Unemployment and underemployment constituted a problem of serious proportions in most ghettos, whereas job creation was scarcely scratching the surface. So far as training was concerned, a careful survey in 1968 concluded: "The most gross estimate indicates that less than 10 percent of persons needing the job training programs can be enrolled in them. . . . Certainly for particular subgroups (slum dwellers, migrants, welfare recipients, deprived youth, etc.) the needs vastly exceed the available resources."[33]

There was no lack of programs. The 1968 study found thirty-one different job training programs, administered by about twenty different federal agencies authorized by about a dozen different laws.[34] One wonders whether such a multiplicity of programs might not make for administrative chaos. In a message to the Congress in August 1969 President Richard M. Nixon proposed "a

[32] See *Special Analyses, Budget of the United States Government, Fiscal Year 1970,* "Special Analysis K."

[33] Greenleigh Associates, Inc., *Opening the Doors: Job Training Programs,* Pt. 2, *Text and Tables:* A Report to the Committee on Administration of Training Programs (Government Printing Office, 1968), p. 62.

[34] *Ibid.,* p. 13.

comprehensive new Manpower Training Act that would pull together much of the array of Federal training services and make it possible for State and local government to respond to the needs of the individual trainee." The message argued that the multitude of existing programs, combined with inflexible funding arrangements, had led to inefficient and ineffective delivery of manpower training services.[35] This may indeed be part of the problem, but a committee that made a detailed study of United States manpower programs reported to the secretary of health, education, and welfare that the lack of adequate funding was much more important than administrative defects in accounting for the limited impact of the programs.[36]

Even if present manpower programs (or the proposed consolidation) were funded at reasonable levels, there is considerable room for doubt concerning how effective they would be at removing people from poverty. There is evidence that training programs that work quite well for those who have had fairly good employment records in the past do not work as well for the hard-core unemployed and ghetto youth, who are the people most in need of improving their situation in the job market.[37] A study made for the Congress by the comptroller general concluded that most of the manpower programs associated with the war on poverty "experienced high, early dropout rates which strongly indicated that many enrollees received little or no actual help."[38] Although this probably overstates the case, in that many of those who stayed probably did receive some help, there can be no doubt that the problem of dropouts is very real and that manpower programs for the poor have not shown either as much promise or performance as might have been hoped.

This is not to say that the effort should be abandoned. It is to say, however, that some of the methods used to retrain previously

---

[35] *Message from the President of the United States Relative to Manpower Training,* Aug. 12, 1969, H. Doc. 91–147, 91 Cong. 1 sess. (1969).

[36] *Report of the Committee on Administration of Training Programs* (CATP, 1968), p. 27.

[37] See Thomas I. Ribich, *Education and Poverty* (Brookings Institution, 1968).

[38] *Review of Economic Opportunity Programs,* by the Comptroller General of the United States, 91 Cong. 1 sess. (1969), p. 9.

successful semiskilled workers are probably not directly applicable to the hard-core unemployed. There was implicit recognition of this by manpower policy makers as reflected by a substantial increase in On-the-Job Training (OJT) programs over several years; expenditures increased from almost zero in 1964 to an estimated $301 million (serving 285,000 persons) in fiscal 1969.[39] On-the-job training programs were being run under the auspices of MDTA, New Careers, Special Impact, and—perhaps most important—JOBS. It was hoped that OJT, combined with local community planning through the Concentrated Employment Program (CEP) and the Cooperative Area Manpower Planning System (CAMPS),[40] would provide better services to the hard-core unemployed than could be provided through institutional training.

As of early 1970, in any case, the only possible conclusion was that manpower policy was contributing minimally to the elimination of poverty. There was general agreement about the need for jobs as well as for meaningful training, and the centrality of the job role should be obvious. But the thinking must be in terms of hundreds of thousands, not tens of thousands, of new jobs. The cheapest jobs that can be created in the public sector would cost just about a billion dollars annually for each 200,000, or $5,000 per job. Although the JOBS program and other OJT efforts are somewhat cheaper than this and should be encouraged to do what they can, their contributions cannot be large unless there are new jobs created in quantity. These realities must be faced if manpower policy is to make its contribution. A few thousand jobs, or a call to private enterprise, simply will not do it.

[39] *Special Analyses, Budget of the United States Government, Fiscal Year 1970,* p. 138.

[40] These two programs are described in Chap. 7.

CHAPTER VI

Income Maintenance

Even the best of manpower and related programs cannot, by themselves, be of much help to individuals and families who are unable to make use of the opportunities presented, or who should not do so until they have improved their capabilities. Such people include most of the aged, many in families headed by a woman, including the woman, and the handicapped. They also include some able-bodied men who, for their own and society's welfare, ought not to take the first (usually dead-end) income-earning opportunity presented to them.

These people need income, either permanently to allow them to live in decency, or temporarily until they can obtain the necessary work training, education, health restoration, or growth, so that they can earn a living. Such income is provided through what are called income maintenance plans—they come in many varieties. The essential feature of these income payments or "transfers" is that they are paid out without the receipt of a good or service in return.

In United States fiscal matters, income maintenance has long been an important element. Much of it is not aimed at the poor, though such transfers are important in the financial life of the poor and ought to become more important. In the mid-1960s such payments totaled "$36 billion per year and go to over 30 million people. This class of income . . . is 40 per cent of the income of the poor population, yet most of it goes to the nonpoor, and at least half the poor do not receive any of it."[1] One example of a transfer payment not designed primarily for the poor is the cash benefits which go to veterans, some of whom may happen to be poor but many of whom are not. Welfare payments, on the other hand, certainly ought to go only to the poor.

Our concern, clearly, is with income maintenance as it affects the poverty population, either by ameliorating the lot of the poor or by raising their incomes enough to remove them from poverty. What should income maintenance do for them? It should augment or supply income for those unable to earn enough to live in decency, and it should do so without destroying the incentive of those receiving it to become nonpoor through their own efforts. On both counts the present system is deficient.

This matter of incentive needs a further word. The poverty population is often considered as comprising two kinds, the unemployables and the employables. The former—husbandless mothers and many of the aged—are largely outside the labor market. For them there is no incentive problem because in general society is not interested in enticing them into employment. For the employables, however, the story is presumed to be different, where they are either unemployed or underemployed (that is, working part time, or full time at a substandard wage). Here the problem is that if the income maintenance is not very carefully devised, the recipient tends to view the income as an alternative to work, and will choose such income in preference to work and income. This will have two adverse effects: it will diminish total output, leaving society less well off than before, and it will tend to reinforce personality traits, such as laziness, that are of little economic or social value.

Actually, very little is known about the operation of incentive. Many people work very hard with little or no monetary incentive, and many poor people must prefer work to the boredom of waiting for the relief check. Perhaps, for the poor, the uncertainties and delays involved in having welfare payments reinstituted argue against taking a low-paying job with an uncertain future more than any matter of pure incentive. In any case, some income

---

[1] Robert J. Lampman, "Ends and Means in the War on Poverty," in Leo Fishman (ed.), *Poverty amid Affluence* (Yale University Press, 1966), p. 221.

maintenance plans now operative seem calculated to destroy whatever incentive may have existed, and these badly need overhaul-
ing.

Existing Programs

We turn now to a brief examination of the principal federal income maintenance programs in the United States. The first operative legislation on the federal level was the Social Security Act of
1935. The old-age insurance and the unemployment compensation
provisions, which were at the center of the original legislation, were
not aimed at the poor, though the poor have benefited from them
greatly in the intervening years. Since these provisions had insurance aspects, it was recognized that they would take effect at a
later time; meanwhile, some emergency provisions of the act were
expected to take care of those who could prove they were needy. It
was expected that these emergency provisions—public assistance, as
they are known—would wither away over time as the insurance
schemes became fully operative.

Although old-age assistance is now declining slowly, other forms
of public assistance are growing, and to this day public assistance
is the single most important income maintenance plan for the non-
aged poor. These transfers failed to wither away because the insurance features of the Social Security Act have never become substantial enough to take care of people who had essentially no other
resources, and some kinds of income loss are not insurable. Furthermore, and implicit in the idea of insurance, the size of payments was closely related to the work experience and earnings history of the insured. Accordingly, the poor, whose work experience
was typically less than average, found that payments were pitifully
low. For example, while nine out of ten who reach the age of sixty-
five are now covered by old-age insurance, the 1970 minimum
benefit of $55 per month is a long way from keeping out of pov-
erty a person whose other resources are minimal or nonexistent.

Under the public assistance provisions, federal funds are transferred to the states for payments to needy individuals and for administrative expenses in connection with the operation of the programs. Broad requirements are established by federal law but

much latitude is permitted, and the welfare system must be regarded as essentially a series of state systems. The federal contribution is greater, at least proportionally, in those states having low per capita income.[2]

Public assistance has six components: old-age assistance (OAA), aid to the blind (AB), aid to the permanently and totally disabled (APTD), general assistance (GA), and two types of aid to families with dependent children (AFDC and AFDC-UP; UP denotes unemployed parents). Of these, AB and APTD have been small and remain so. OAA was by far the dominant type of assistance until recently; it has finally begun to decline in importance as old-age insurance has become nearly universal and more generous, although OAA remains financially significant. AFDC has grown rapidly in recent years and shows no sign of slowing down; it is now the largest part of public assistance. It has also changed its nature somewhat; at first its clients were chiefly widowed women with children, but now deserted and unwed mothers are the typical clients. AFDC-UP is authorized by the 1967 social security amendments. It permits states to make AFDC payments to help support children whose parents are unemployed, even if the father is present. Only half of the states have started such programs, and two states, New York and California, account for two-thirds of the money spent.[3]

Total expenditures (cash and payment for services) on public assistance are now $10 billion annually, and the total number of recipients is 10 million per year. With the advent of Medicaid in 1965, a new category of assistance loomed as an important element in the picture. In 1968 over $317 million was spent monthly on medical aid for perhaps 5 million medically indigent persons. All of the programs except general assistance are "categorical." To be eligible it is not enough to be poor. One must be poor and also fit into another category: blind, a mother, aged, or disabled. All of the states have GA programs, but in every case they are very

[2] See Ida C. Merriam and Alfred M. Skolnik, *Social Welfare Expenditures Under Public Programs in the United States, 1929–66,* Social Security Administration (1968), p. 75.

[3] *Welfare in Review,* Vol. 7 (May–June 1969), p. 52.

small, accounting for only about 7 percent of public assistance payments.[4] AFDC does nothing for the poor without children and, where AFDC-UP is not operative, provides strong disincentives to work and to family stability.

The categorical aspect of the welfare system deserves some emphasis. Many categories are not neat; that is, it is not simple to determine whether a person is or is not in a given one. Furthermore, as circumstances change, a person may be in at one moment and out at another. In order to determine eligibility, therefore, an initial examination and frequent reexaminations of the individual circumstances are required. This is done by the 35,000 caseworkers located in states and local agencies across the country.[5] Customarily there is a visit to each client at least once each six months; in many cases visits are more frequent. In January 1969, the secretary of health, education, and welfare issued new regulations to streamline this process, making use of affidavits and spot checks of clients.[6] The plan is being tested in each state; if it is finally implemented, it should mean a substantial improvement in the system.

Determination of what the welfare payment should be is a difficult and sometimes arbitrary proceeding; this is the procedure known as the means test. In theory, each state has determined the amounts required by families of various sizes, and the payment is the difference between the appropriate amount and any resources the client has. But the process is not as simple as that, and frequently visits by the caseworker may result in a $2 increase or decrease in the weekly check. In one case the budget had contained money for haircuts for the children; when it was discovered that the mother was cutting their hair, the payments were reduced by the amount of the budget item!

This is an expensive business. Caseworkers ought to be helping their clients; instead they worry about nickels and dimes in the benefit checks. In 1968, 10 percent of the cost of welfare was administrative (social security administrative costs amount to 2 per-

[4] *Ibid.,* pp. 33, 34.

[5] *Income Maintenance Programs,* Hearings before the Subcommittee on Fiscal Policy of the Joint Economic Committee, 90 Cong. 2 sess. (1968), Vol 2: *Appendix Materials,* p. 698.

[6] *New York Times,* Jan. 19, 1969.

cent).[7] But there are more important costs than the monetary ones. These are the moral costs that go with the personal indignities inherent in close supervision of the lives of clients. This has found its extreme in the "midnight raids" to be sure there is not a surreptitious man in the house of an AFDC client.[8] A large portion of the caseworker-client relation, which should be one of warm cooperation, has turned into an adversary one characterized by concealment, snooping, personal indignity and domination, and chiseling. It is not a happy situation, and it continues to deteriorate as AFDC, which is the worst program in this regard, continues to become quantitatively more important in the total picture.

These nonmonetary costs may become higher as a result of the 1967 amendments to the Social Security Act, which strengthen the hand of the caseworker even more. It is now possible to force relief clients, on pain of having payments cut off entirely, to put children in day care centers and enter job training. This extreme measure reflects a growing dissatisfaction with the operation of the welfare system, though it would appear that the dissatisfaction is moving the system in just the wrong direction.[9]

The moral degradation that has become so much a part of the system is one of the important elements leading to its indictment, but there are several others. One is the great and essentially arbitrary variability among states in the size of payments. Average monthly OAA payments in June 1968 were $36.05 in Mississippi, $107.70 in New Hampshire. Mississippi paid $44.50 monthly to its permanently and totally disabled, Iowa $128.00.[10] The differences

[7] U.S. Department of Health, Education, and Welfare, Social and Rehabilitation Service, National Center for Social Statistics, "Public Assistance: Costs of State and Local Administration, Services, and Training" (1968; processed), Table 12, and "Source of Funds Expended for Public Assistance Payments and for the Cost of Administration, Services, and Training" (1968; processed), Table 1; Robert J. Myers, "Administrative Expenses of the Social Security Program," *Social Security Bulletin,* Vol. 32 (September 1969), p. 23.

[8] Fortunately these have now been ruled unconstitutional. See *Welfare in Review,* Vol. 7 (March–April 1969), p. 35.

[9] Unfortunately, the Family Assistance Plan proposed in 1969 by President Nixon, if adopted, would reinforce these provisions. The plan is discussed later in this chapter.

[10] Wilbur J. Cohen, "A Ten-Point Program To Abolish Poverty," *Social Security Bulletin,* Vol. 31 (December 1968), p. 10.

are accounted for largely by the different wealth of the states, though the federal government, as mentioned above, has done some equalizing. Migration from the poor to the richer states has also brought about some equalizing, but this sort of equalization is of doubtful social utility. The point is that poverty is not really a state matter; it is a national disease.

Eligibility requirements differ among states in the same arbitrary manner as payment sizes. For example, the disabled in Colorado are apparently those who are unable to work; in California dependency on another individual is required. States have varying definitions of need. Two poor persons in different states must wonder, if they ever compare notes, just what the accident of geography has to do with determining their eligibility.[11]

There is another obvious defect in public assistance. It does not cover enough people, and it does not provide enough for most of those who are covered. The 10 million people who receive public assistance comprise about 40 percent of the poverty population. In many states the maximum allowable public assistance payment comes to only a fraction of the amount established by the federal definition of poverty, and in only a few does it come near that amount.

Finally, and perhaps most important of all, public assistance seems unable to cope with the incentive problem. The means test determines the level of payment by subtracting the client's resources from the state standard. If earned income rises, the public assistance payment is reduced by the same amount, so that total income is unchanged. There is, in other words, an implicit 100 percent tax imposed on the individual until the earned income exceeds the minimum requirement used by the particular state. Since most public assistance recipients have only low-wage options in the labor market, when they have any at all, monetary incentive to work is essentially nonexistent.

In 1962 and again in 1967 the Congress recognized this problem

[11] Residence requirements of varying duration were in force in all states except New York until they were invalidated by the Supreme Court in early 1969; *New York Times,* April 22, 1969. For eligibility requirements by states, see U.S. Department of Health, Education, and Welfare, Social and Rehabilitation Service, Assistance Payments Administration, *Characteristics of State Public Assistance Plans Under the Social Security Act,* 1967 ed. (1969).

by permitting states to allow some earned income to be disregarded in calculating public assistance payments.[12] At present the first $30 per month and one-third of additional income for a family on AFDC is so treated. This has not solved the problem; fortunately the problem is attracting more and more attention as one with which the government must come to grips.[13]

Some of the problems could be dealt with by changes in the public assistance laws and procedures. Federal standards, for example, could be imposed more widely. But the categorical nature of the aid seems to bring necessarily the evils of individual budgeting, means testing, and supervision which are behind so many of the problems. It may well be that some entirely new ideas are needed.

Before describing alternative income maintenance systems, let us summarize the principal drawbacks of public assistance as it exists. Any system that replaces public assistance, whether in whole or in part, must avoid most or all of these negative aspects. There are four principal characteristics to be avoided. First is the indignity that goes with the means test, plus the elaborate and wasteful administrative apparatus that seems to be required in its administration and enforcement. Second is the built-in incentive against earning income or against family unity included in most of the present assistance programs. Third, variations among states in payments, eligibility, and so on make no sense in a national system. Finally, public assistance is not reaching enough of the poor—three-fifths of them at any one time are outside the system, subsisting in ways we do not understand.

Public assistance could be changed to overcome most of these negative features. Indeed, experiments are being made or proposed for substituting an affidavit on income for the laborious budget making now practiced by the social worker. And, as was pointed out, in 1962 and 1967 the welfare laws were amended to permit states to allow some earnings without deduction in welfare payments. One change frequently suggested is the establish-

---

[12] 76 Stat. 207; 81 Stat. 881.
[13] See, for example, *"Having the Power, We Have the Duty,"* Report to the secretary of health, education, and welfare by the U.S. Advisory Council on Public Welfare (June 1966).

ment of national norms, in order to eliminate some of the variation among states. All these changes are in the right direction. Once some sort of consensus has been achieved on a preferred system, whether to get there by instituting an entirely new system or by changing the existing one is largely a matter of tactics. To an examination of two new possibilities we now turn.

The Family Allowance

Family allowance plans are widely used throughout the world; the United States is one of the few modern industrialized nations without one. Such plans make grants to families, usually varying in amount with the number of children. Details differ, but most such plans disregard income entirely in determining eligibility, making the payments to rich and poor alike. The justification for this is that the formative years of childhood are extremely important in the subsequent development of the individual. Many families are in a period of low income while their children are young, and therefore these grants come at a time of need.

Most family allowance proposals would classify the grants as taxable income, and would repeal the income tax exemption for children eligible for the grant. Those whose incomes are at or above the tax-paying level would receive less than the full grant, and those in the highest brackets would find their disposable income decreased. In the lowest bracket, for example, a family with one eligible child would have its taxable income increased by the amount of one exemption, or $600; at the 14 percent tax rate for that bracket, the family's income tax would be increased by $84 per year, and it would benefit on balance by the excess of the allowance over the $84.[14] A family in the 50 percent marginal bracket would need an allowance of $300 in order to break even.

People in the United States with children already have a form of family allowance through the dependency exemption in the income tax structure. The important exception is the family whose income is not large enough to be taxable. This is the family that would benefit most from a family allowance; it would retain the

[14] Calculations are based on the Revenue Act of 1964, 78 Stat. 19.

whole amount or, in the case of those pushed above the tax limit by the allowance, somewhat less than the whole, but in any case more than the family with higher income (except for the mythical family that stood exactly to the penny on the threshold of paying taxes before the institution of the family allowances).

Any universal scheme of this sort would have significant financial implications. Alvin Schorr, an authority on family allowances, has costed a plan that would pay $10 per month for the first child and $40 per month for all subsequent ones until they reach the age of eighteen. Forty dollars was used because it was just above the AFDC average payment per child. Such a plan would reduce social security and other assistance programs, and increase tax receipts, all of which would offset the gross cost of the payments. The income tax exemption for children would be repealed and the allowance would be taxable. The net annual cost would come to about $14 billion.[15]

A second possibility would be more modest. This would be a benefit of $50 per month payable for each child under six, again with tax exemptions eliminated for all children and with the payment to be regarded as taxable. This plan would reach all children under six (25 million in 1964), and indirectly some older children in families with children under six. The gross cost would be $14.9 billion annually, to be offset by $2 billion of taxes collected on that income and $7 billion from the elimination of the exemption for children. The net, therefore, would be $5.9 billion annually. It is difficult to calculate, but this proposal would apparently remove from poverty something less than half the poor families with children under six and would substantially help the other half.

This proposal might see a substantial number of these families slide back into poverty when the last child reached the age of six. While its proponents would prefer not to see the payments stop at

---

[15] Based on data for the mid-1960s, when there were 70 million children in the United States living in families. See Alvin L. Schorr, *Poor Kids* (Basic Books, 1966), in particular Chap. 9. I have borrowed heavily from this work, including the examples presented here. During a year of close professional association, many of Mr. Schorr's ideas became mine as well. My intellectual debt to him is great, even though we retain a cordial disagreement about the relative merits of family allowances and a negative income tax.

that point, they argue that if we are faced with hard choices for financial reasons, there is a case that the years when preschool children are in the family are of unusual importance. The point can also be made that when a child reaches the age of six, society begins spending large amounts on him in other ways—mainly for education.

There are also substantial income distribution effects to be derived from implementing such proposals. In the one just described, a family would receive $600 per year for six years for one child but would give up an exemption for eighteen years. This works out, at tax rates based on the Revenue Act of 1964, to a break-even point at about $12,000 of net taxable income, where the marginal tax rate is 25 percent. For each child the family receives $600 a year, $450 after taxes, for six years, a total of $2,700; without the allowance the same family would save $150 a year in taxes for eighteen years, a total of $2,700. Above that point disposable income is reduced; below, it is increased. Those paying no tax would benefit most, but there would also be some benefits for the nonpoor.

One obvious question to ask about family allowance plans is the impact to be expected on the birth rate, since a reduced birth rate has been viewed as essential to the long-run elimination of poverty. A great deal of careful research has been done on this matter; the conclusion seems to be that there is no hard evidence of a causal link between the payment of family allowances and a rise in the birth rates among these beneficiaries.[16] There have been periods when birth rates have fallen and when they have risen, both while family allowances were in effect. It is not possible to be certain that birth rates might have risen less rapidly or fallen more rapidly without these payments, but it is clear that the reverse is far from established.

Perhaps the most persuasive evidence is the experience of Canada, where a family allowance plan with fairly small payments was adopted in 1944. Every effort was made to follow the impact of the plan on the birth rate. The birth rate moved downward during the depression of the 1930s, upward during and after the Second World War, and has been falling since 1957. The adoption of the plan in 1944 was thus followed by a rapid increase in births. But

[16] *Ibid.*, pp. 66–73.

close examination indicates that the increase did not result from adoption of a family allowance and that it is much more likely that Canada, like other countries, reacted to the general buoyancy of the postwar period. Most telling of all, Schorr plotted the variations in U.S. birth rates beside those in Canada for 1926–62; the two behaved almost identically, though Canada instituted family allowances in the forties and the United States did not.[17] It appears to be recognized that making a living by having more children is doing it the hard way.

How does the family allowance notion measure up, particularly in relation to the deficiencies that have become part of the present public assistance system? It certainly rates high for eliminating any means test. No stigma could possibly attach to it as far as any one person or family is concerned, since all families or large classes of them would be eligible. Similarly, it is unlikely that the suggested version of a family allowance would substantially impair incentive to work. Every worker would retain all of any increased earnings he enjoyed, except as he might become subject to income tax, which would not be attributable in any case to the family allowance. The grant could be thought of as the inverse of a head tax, which is widely regarded as having the least effect of any tax on the incentive to work. It is conceivable (but only barely) that someone would give up working overtime, say, when the family allowance became available, but this could hardly happen enough to be noticeable. Adverse incentives arise when added income is taxed away either explicitly or implicitly, in whole or in part, and on this count any variation on the family allowance plan comes off very well indeed.

The plan has a number of drawbacks. One is simply that the payments suddenly stop one day—to be sure when the child reaches a certain age—but it is not realistic to think that a sudden cut in expenses will be coordinated with the stoppage. For persons and families living close to the subsistence line, this adjustment is bound to be painful more often than not. This would be a feature of any scheme based on other than simple income deficiency. Children and income deficiency are no doubt related, but the relationship is less precise than this plan implies.

[17] *Ibid.*, p. 69.

Another defect, perhaps, is that money will go to the nonpoor, the amounts depending on the financial details of any particular variant. But, at the tax rates used in the example, some will go to the nonpoor whenever the annual allowance is greater than $84 per child, as it surely would be. This could be changed, but not without altering the idea in a quite fundamental way. There is no harm in some subsidy to the nonpoor, but it does reduce the impact on the poor of each dollar spent. This is also a feature of many variations of the negative income tax, which is discussed in the following section.[18]

A third problem is that it makes no provision for the poor who are childless. People with children have no monopoly on poverty, and it can be argued that a plan as ambitious as most family allowances are should provide for all the needy, or be capable of doing so. This criticism rests on the fact that family allowances are aimed at children first and then at poor children, so perhaps it is not preeminently a poverty program. The question, presumably, is whether the overlap, which is clearly great, is great enough.

A closely allied deficiency is that the payment is the same to the very poor as to the not-so-poor. This means that it cannot relieve the poverty of the poorest (even those with children) without overpaying the not-so-poor by substantial amounts. Again this is because the payments are not geared to the extent of poverty of the given family, as public assistance is and as the negative income tax is. How important this is may be a matter of taste, and in the long run the emphasis on children may do much toward eliminating poverty, but it is well to understand that the characteristic exists. It can be argued, and the writer subscribes to this view, that this is a defect in an expensive weapon against poverty.[19]

[18] A political point of some significance is that the appeal, and thus the political palatability, of the family allowance would be enhanced by its broad clientele; this might increase the probability of its adoption in preference to a negative tax system.

[19] In a study of family allowances in five other countries, Martin Schnitzer makes just this point. He concludes: "The family allowance does not appear to be a particularly efficient [measure] . . . when considered as an anti-poverty device [in the United States]." "The Family Allowance," in *Income Maintenance Programs*, Vol. 2: *Appendix Materials*, p. 528.

The Negative Income Tax

In its 1966 report the Council of Economic Advisers, after discussing some of the shortcomings of public assistance, pointed out that "another approach is the institution of uniformly determined payments to families based only on the amount by which their incomes fall short of minimum subsistence levels. Such a system could be integrated with the existing income tax system. This plan is now receiving intensive study by many scholars."[20]

The plan that the council was referring to was one that has come to be called the negative income tax.[21] The idea is not new, and has found support among both conservative and liberal elements.[22] As the council suggested, it has been widely studied and discussed in recent years, and there are those who think it may well be the next major social welfare innovation in the United States. There is an appealing simplicity about the idea, a simplicity incidentally which may be misleading in the event. There are also some who regard the idea as wildly impractical.

The negative income tax and the family allowance plan are regarded as competitive proposals, and rightly so. By and large, they are both techniques for getting money payments to the disadvantaged. But if poverty and low income can be equated, then the negative income tax can go farther in its comprehensive form toward the elimination of poverty than any other plan; indeed, it can go all the way. Its benefits go directly to the poor, and for each poor person the benefits vary in proportion to his poverty. In this

[20] *Economic Report of the President, January 1966,* p. 115.

[21] To the chagrin of many of its supporters, who would prefer a more appealing name but have been unable to invent one that will stick.

[22] Some 1,300 economists at almost 150 institutions signed a petition to the Congress in 1968 urging adoption of "a national system of income guarantees and supplements." *Income Maintenance Programs,* Vol. 2: *Appendix Materials,* pp. 676–90. In addition, the President's Commission on Income Maintenance Programs recommended the adoption of a negative income tax in its final report, *Poverty amid Plenty: The American Paradox* (1969), p. 7.

sense the plan would seem to be the ultimate weapon in the anti-poverty arsenal.[23]

The negative income tax is a broadly conceived income mainte-nance scheme. Payments are made on the basis of the income re-ceived by a family in a specific period. If the family has no income, it receives the "minimum income guarantee" as a transfer pay-ment. If the family receives some income, the transfer payment is reduced by some proportion of the earned income; the proportion of reduction is called the "negative tax rate." At some level of in-come, the transfer payment becomes zero. Above this "break-even point" the family will presumably pay taxes (receive negative transfers). Thus for negative rates less than 100 percent, as earned income rises total disposable income also rises, though at a slower rate. This feature allows for positive work incentives.

A potentially important feature of the scheme is, as its name im-plies, its relation to the present income tax system. The positive system taxes incomes above a given level defined by standard ex-emptions and deductions. This seems to imply that this level of resources is necessary for basic needs and should not be taxed.[24] Income above this level is taxed at progressively higher rates. If a family's income is below the level necessary for basic needs, how-ever, it does not now receive any assistance via the tax mechanism in meeting these needs. While a nonpoor family is assured that the income required to meet its basic needs will not be taxed away, the basic income needs of the low-income family are in no way assured. Thus nonpoor families receive considerable advan-tage from the exemptions for their children; personal income tax cuts, as in 1964, help high-income families directly and considera-bly; but poor families receive no direct benefit. A negative income tax scheme would correct this asymmetry by paying a transfer, with the size based on the amount by which income is below some level stated to be necessary for basic requirements. For example,

[23] The welfare message submitted by President Nixon to Congress in August 1969 contained a number of negative income tax features. Details of the proposal are dis-cussed later in this chapter.

[24] This was not the original justification for these deductions, which have not al-ways borne a relation to subsistence levels. But today they approximate the poverty income levels.

the minimum income guarantee might be made equivalent to the standard exemptions and deductions of the positive income tax system.

The negative income tax concept can be applied at whatever level and proceed at whatever rate is chosen. Once the minimum income guarantee and the negative rate (or rates) have been selected, the break-even point is fixed. Or, once a break-even level and a negative rate have been decided on, the minimum guarantee is fixed.[25] In designing a plan, the present exemptions and deductions might be chosen as the minimum income guarantee, as suggested above. This differs somewhat from the poverty line, being well below the mark for individuals and well above that for large families. The two lines are approximately equivalent at the four-person family level. If the exemption-deduction line is chosen, the system will be biased against small family units and in favor of large ones. If the poverty line is chosen, some overlap will occur unless the positive system is adapted to conform to the poverty lines.

Another and possibly helpful way to explain the negative income tax is through a simple graph, as in Figure 1, which shows the relation between preallowance (or pretransfer) income and disposable income for a family of four.[26]

[25] The amount of the transfer payment may be calculated in two ways: (a) subtract the preallowance income from the break-even income and multiply the remainder by the negative rate; or (b) multiply the preallowance income by the negative rate and subtract the product from the minimum guarantee. Preallowance (or pretransfer) income is family income before taxes and transfers.

[26] Disposable income, the income in the hands of the family after transfers and taxes, is the amount which the family is free to spend on goods and services. It shows the effect of a tax and income maintenance system. Preallowance income, as explained above, is family income prior to taxes and transfers; this would be the income base on which the amount of the transfer payments would be calculated. Taxes might be calculated on the same base or on some other. Preallowance income would include earnings, unincorporated business profits, corporate dividends, rents, and probably certain interest income. Social security payments might also be included, in which case the negative tax would supplement social security benefits. Public assistance payments would probably be excluded. The definition of preallowance income would be an important part of the design of a negative income tax system and would almost certainly not be the adjusted gross income of the present positive tax system. For the sake of brevity, we refer simply to "income" in the text.

FIGURE I

Relation of Preallowance Income to Disposable Income
for a Family of Four

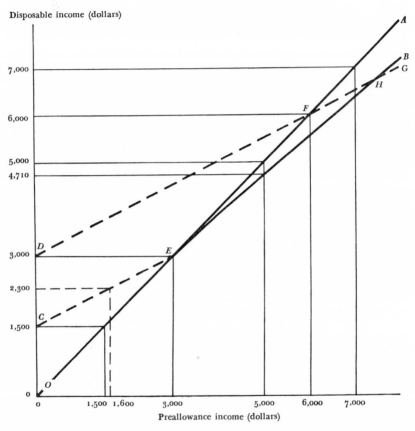

Note: Calculations are based on deductions, exemptions, and rates in the Revenue Act of 1964.

If there were no income taxes, the forty-five degree line *OA* would
depict this relation. That is, a family earning $5,000 would keep
$5,000. But there *are* income taxes. For a family of four using the
minimum standard deduction, taxes would begin at $3,000 at the
lowest rate, 14 percent. Above $3,000, therefore, the family's dis-
posable income is less than its taxable income. For example, if it

earned $5,000, its disposable income would be $4,710.[27] Below $3,000 taxable and disposable income are still equal, so that the curve *OEB* now states the relation at all income levels. To the right of $3,000, the line *OB* is curved rather than straight because the marginal tax rate on incomes rises as incomes rise. The growing distance between *OB* and *OA* as income rises is an indication that the proportion of income paid out as taxes increases as taxable income increases.

The main effect of the negative income tax is to change the situation to the left of point *E;* and there are an infinite number of ways this can be done. Suppose, for example, the nation desired to guarantee a disposable income of at least $3,000 to every family of four. One way to accomplish this would be to set the negative tax rate at 100 percent and the break-even point at $3,000. The curve relating pretransfer and disposable income would then be *DEB*. A family with $2,000 income would receive $1,000 from the Treasury, a family with $1,700 would receive $1,300. The minimum income guarantee would equal the break-even point. Such a version of the negative income tax would, in effect, destroy any incentive to earn income for all those below the established minimum, and for many of those not far above it. For this reason it is not favored by most proponents of the negative income tax.

A more popular variant would set the negative rate at 50 percent. This means that, below a $3,000 break-even income, half the deficit between actual income and $3,000 would be made up. A family with an income of $1,600 would receive an addition of $700[28] so that its total disposable income would be $2,300. A family with no income would receive $1,500, the minimum income guarantee. The appropriate curve in Figure 1 would be CEB.

Some relations can now be seen. If instead of a 50 percent negative rate 33⅓ percent is chosen, the guaranteed minimum would be $1,000, and in this case families would forego subsidy at the rate of one dollar for every three they earned; in the 50 percent case it is one for every two. Other variants are possible. The negative rate does not have to be uniform; it could vary (as does the positive

---

[27] Calculations are based on deductions, exemptions, and rates in the Revenue Act of 1964.

[28] Calculated: 0.5 ($3,000 — $1,600) = $700; or $1,500 — 0.5 ($1,600) = $700.

tax rate) with income, and it could vary in either direction. Some feel that the subsidy should be higher at very low incomes and taper downward as the income approaches the poverty level. All these variants can be accommodated in the general concept of negative income tax, and none has been established as clearly preferable.

The discussion thus far has taken $3,000 for the family of four to be the poverty line and the break-even point. It is evident that at this figure any negative tax rate less than 100 percent will take no one out of poverty. The arithmetic is such that the negative tax does away with some fraction (depending on the rate) of the deficit, but never all of it. Suppose it is desired to use the negative income tax to eliminate poverty as defined. Is there a way to do this?

The answer is yes. It can be done by the 100 percent tax route, as already shown. But the adverse impact on the earning incentive is such as to make this route very unappealing. However, there is another way. Suppose a 50 percent rate is adopted but the break-even line is established at $6,000 rather than at $3,000. This would mean that a family with zero income would receive $3,000 in negative taxes (half of $6,000); with a pretransfer income of $2,000 the family would receive an additional $2,000,[29] and so on. No one would gross less than $3,000, and all additional income earned between zero and $6,000 would reduce the subsidy by half of what was earned. On Figure 1 a new curve is required; it is *DFG*.

Several things need comment. For one, the new curve always slopes upward, which means that at every level of income the family is allowed to keep some of any additional income it earns—there is never an implicit 100 percent tax. For another, this system would pay negative taxes to some families not defined as poor, and who had previously been paying positive taxes—those between *E* and *F* on the figure. For a third, some nonpoor families (those between *F* and *H*) would pay less than before in positive taxes. And finally, the poor (those to the left of *E*) would receive subsidies larger than required to lift them to the poverty line. The impact on those with highest incomes would be generally less than

[29] Calculated: 0.5 ($6,000 − $2,000) = $2,000; or $3,000 − 0.5 ($2,000) = $2,000.

on those with lower incomes, as indicated by the convergence of curves *DFG* and *CEB* as incomes rise. Improvements over the present tax system through transfers by this system would be as shown in Table 7 for four-person families with pretransfer incomes from $0 to $6,000.

TABLE 7

Comparison of Disposable Income for a Family of Four under a Negative Income Tax and under the 1964 Revenue Act

(*In dollars*)

		Disposable income	
Preallowance income	Negative tax subsidy	Under negative tax	Under 1964 Revenue Act
0	3,000	3,000	0
1,000	2,500	3,500	1,000
2,000	2,000	4,000	2,000
3,000	1,500	4,500	3,000
4,000	1,000	5,000	3,860
5,000	500	5,500	4,710
6,000	0	6,000	5,550

This brings us face to face with what might be called the three-way dilemma of negative income tax. If the only interest is in paying small amounts of negative taxes in order to bring low-income people into the extended tax system—which may be a commendable goal—the problem does not arise. But when the system is considered as a major weapon in the war on poverty, there is no way around the dilemma, which has been implicit in the preceding pages. There is a trade-off among the cost of the system (to the Treasury), the level of the minimum income to be guaranteed, and the rates used (which are so important to the strength of incentives). A high guaranteed income rules out low negative rates except at very high cost, and the presumption is that low rates are necessary for the maintenance of incentive. To be specific, if there is a $3,000 guarantee, as in the example, a 50 percent rate means income earners keep half of what they earn and no one pays a positive tax until his income passes $6,000. At the same minimum, if one feels the rate should be one-third so that families may keep 67 cents out of each dollar they earn, a positive tax cannot be imposed on incomes lower than $9,000. This will push up the cost and make it necessary for marginal rates on higher incomes to be considerably steeper, or for the system to be subsidized from some other part of general revenues.

These trade-offs compel compromises in the system, and anyone working out details quickly becomes aware of the problem. They suggest the need for experimenting with rates higher than would be considered appropriate a priori, or using a minimum income lower than ideal. The requirement is to keep the curve in Figure 1 always sloping upward to the right, with the assumption that the greater the slope, the greater the incentive of the system. One redeeming feature is that the negative tax payment declines as income rises, so that it tends to bulk highest for those who are below or not far above the poverty line. Considering how conservative the definition of poverty is, it follows that a subsidy to those marginally above the line is hardly to be regarded as totally inappropriate. And a glance at Figure 1 will indicate that the negative tax payments made to those below the poverty line are several times the payments to those above the line. (In the example used here, they are just three times as great.)

It is worth stressing that the system involves a number of unknowns. Something can be learned by experimentation; a negative income tax experiment was initiated in August 1968 in several cities in New Jersey.[30] Also, no negative income tax would be instituted in comprehensive form all at once. Presumably, if it won favor, it would be instituted gradually. The next time a tax cut was put into effect, part of it would be in the form of some negative rates, probably along with reductions in the positive rates. Later it could be expanded when the next cut became appropriate. As this took place, the effect on incentive could be watched, and the system could be revised as experience was gained.

The aged poor would benefit from a negative income tax. There are 5 million of them, many receiving payments under the

[30] *Income Maintenance Programs,* Hearings, Vol. 2, p. 463. The experiment is described in Harold Watts, "Graduated Work Incentives: An Experiment in Negative Taxation," *American Economic Review,* Vol. 59 (May 1969), pp. 463–78.

old-age, survivors, and disability insurance program (OASDI).[31] These benefits could be raised, but only—as the system is now administered—if they were raised across the board, for poor and nonpoor alike; this would be very expensive. An estimate made in 1966 was that it would take $11 billion to remove half the aged poor from poverty by an across-the-board increase in social security benefits, even though the poverty gap for the aged is only $3 billion.[32] Under a negative income tax, the poor could report their social security payments as pretransfer income, and negative payments would then apply. Effectively, OAA would be replaced but not OASDI, which is a going, well-financed system, and the problem of the aged poor could probably be solved. Unemployment compensation payments could be treated in the same way as OASDI benefits.

Merits of the Negative Income Tax

There are a number of very real advantages inherent in the negative income tax, particularly when it is compared with public assistance or a family allowance system. One of these is the simplicity of the idea. It is an extension of a highly viable existing tax system; it involves periodically filling out and filing a form stating what one's income is, a procedure already followed by many of the families and individuals concerned. The Treasury already receives income statements from about 75 million units; under the negative income tax system there would be a few million more. The Treasury already sends out millions of income tax refund checks each year.

It might be that the Social Security Administration should be designated to handle negative tax payments—that administration is already in touch with many of the prospective clients. Both the Social Security Administration and the Internal Revenue Service

---

[31] U.S. Bureau of the Census, *Current Population Reports,* Series P-20, No. 189, "Selected Characteristics of Persons and Families: March 1969" (1969), p. 7.

[32] Christopher Green, *Negative Taxes and the Poverty Problem* (Brookings Institution, 1967), p. 42. The poverty gap is the total sum of money which, if ideally distributed, would place all the relevant poor just above their poverty lines.

are highly skilled at processing large quantities of financial reports and issuing large numbers of checks. After a tooling-up period, either agency would probably take the new program in stride.

Another attractive feature of the negative income tax is its automatic nature. As low incomes rise, the payments decline and then stop when the break-even point is reached—no one has to make a finding that the family's situation has improved. And when income falls, new families automatically become eligible, and payments rise all along the line. This is part of the ease and simplicity of administration. Also, it would become a very effective countercyclical device—payments to the public would rise when incomes decline and vice versa.

A third advantage is basic. The sole criterion for negative tax payments would be need, measured by income and family size. If these are valid measures (and there will be cases where they are not), then by definition the payments would go where they were needed. As has been seen, however, a comprehensive program designed to eliminate poverty would see some payments going to the nonpoor, and to some extent this would have to be regarded as a weakening of this advantage.

Under the present public assistance system payments are almost tailor-made for each recipient family. Public assistance is designed to insure that each family is able to buy a certain basic market basket of goods, no matter what the cost. The system does not usually accomplish this purpose, but it is designed to do so. The negative income tax scheme, in contrast, does not tie payments to a basic market basket. Rather, cash payments are varied only by family size and income level. A family of a given size and income would receive the same payment whether it lived in Biloxi or in San Francisco. The transfer might buy a handsome basket in Biloxi but only a smaller amount in San Francisco.[33] Migration from areas of opportunity (San Francisco) might thus be encouraged. The poor in San Francisco would seem to be treated unfairly. One of the problems in defining the poverty line is in confronting geo-

[33] Again it may be noted that the availability of more free public services in San Francisco than in Biloxi would compensate to some extent and thus moderate the degree of "unfairness" to the poor in San Francisco.

graphical differences in costs of living. It can well be argued that a
negative income tax institutionalizes geographical inequity and
that only a personalized public assistance approach can avoid this
problem. It is just this personalized treatment, however, that
seems to be the key problem with public assistance.

Although public assistance payments are made largely in cash,
the constant supervision and adjustment of the allowance deprives
the payments of many of the qualities of income. First, one's
choices of what to do with the money are limited. In most states a
car may not be owned. One would probably not want to save,
since a bank account might be counted as a resource next month.
Second, the receipt of a public assistance allowance is often visible,
since social worker visits are associated with it. The recipient must
assume an inferior position with respect to his peers as well as to
the social worker, and thus public assistance carries with it a degree of social stigma. The cash allowance, then, is less valuable
than an equal cash income, and the personalized mechanism that
is necessary to provide a basic market basket of goods seems to be a
greater disadvantage than geographical inequities.

Negative income tax payments would be pure income with no
restriction, and without stigma, since for all practical purposes
they are invisible. Such a transfer payment would be nearly equivalent to any other kind of income. While it would be hoped that a
negative tax payment would be adequate to buy most of a basic
market basket, its relation to that market basket is of less importance than the fact that a minimum status in society would be
guaranteed.

A final advantage is that the negative income tax safeguards economic incentives. It is possible to devise systems under which families always retain a part of additional earnings, no matter what
the level of income. For that part of the low-income population
that is employed or employable, this is presumably a matter of
considerable importance; "presumably," because all too little is
known about the relation between the desire for income and the
desire for leisure, whether at low-income levels or high. Gallaway
thinks he has demonstrated that those over sixty-five will substitute leisure for work when public payments become available, but

whether this can be extrapolated to the rest of the population is questionable.[34] Also, the impact of a 50 percent implicit tax as against a 100 percent tax is still very imperfectly understood.

But it is probable that the political acceptability of the plan would require a built-in incentive for the employable group, and it can be so constructed. For the nonemployables this matter is of much less importance. For them, the naïve form of guaranteed income scheme discussed earlier would be quite satisfactory, but so would the plan with incentives built in. The incentive plan would not hurt those for whom it is not relevant while it would provide positive incentives to those for whom it is. As time passes and as programs of training and education reach more and more people, the employed and employables remaining in poverty should become a smaller and smaller portion of the total. This will be enlarged on later in the chapter.

It is well to emphasize the relation between income maintenance and work incentive. A zero tax rate, as prevails at low-income levels under the present income tax system, maximizes work incentive by allowing the workman to keep all of each dollar earned. The zero rate, however, has no welfare value. A 100 percent negative tax rate, as under AFDC before July 1, 1969, maximizes income maintenance by insuring a specific level of income no matter what level is earned. The 100 percent rate, as has been noted, has no work incentive value. Work incentives operate to maximize current national product. Income maintenance operates, as was outlined early in this chapter, to increase future national product and present national welfare. In adopting a general transfer system, society must choose some combination of these goals, establishing minimum income guarantees and negative rates accordingly.

Drawbacks of the Negative Income Tax

Before we completely embrace the negative income tax, we had better pause and take a look at some of the problems it would bring.

[34] Lowell E. Gallaway, "Negative Income Tax Rates and the Elimination of Poverty," *National Tax Journal*, Vol. 19 (September 1966), pp. 298–307.

While the system has great promise as a weapon in the war on poverty and is preferable to other income maintenance proposals, it ought to be stressed that it is as yet untried and needs more study. Even before that, however, some knotty problems are visible.

First there is a question about frequency of payment. Today most tax payments by the individual are made effectively each payday through withholding by the employer. Tax settlements and refunds are made annually. The people who are to benefit from the negative income tax are people who need money promptly and frequently—probably biweekly or at least monthly. This will increase the administrative costs of the tax system considerably and means that it is not appropriate when calculating the administrative burden of the plan to think of negative tax recipients as simple additions to the number on the income tax rolls. This is one of the considerations that suggests that the Social Security Administration may have more relevant experience than the Internal Revenue Service and might be best equipped to administer the program.

Under a negative income tax, it would probably be necessary for the poor to estimate their income at the beginning of the tax year. For some this will not be a problem but, particularly for those casually employed, the variability and the importance of chance factors would be such as to make estimating within tolerable limits a difficult task. This could mean frequent changes in the estimates, thus again complicating the bookkeeping requirements. More important, it would mean many year-end settlements, and for this population settlements in favor of the government might create real hardship or even be impossible to make. This could pose severe problems for the integrity of the system.

There is also the matter of possible fraud. Presumably the administrators would accept a certification of income and dependents, as is done now at the positive end of the income tax system. There would no doubt have to be spot checks and it is probable that some negative taxes would be paid out against dishonest claims which would escape detection. Some fear that fraud would be widespread; others doubt that it would approach the magnitude of present tax evasion by the nonpoor. Nonetheless, it is a possibility, and if suspicion of chiseling were to become widespread it might have serious repercussions on the entire income tax structure. Many people would regard the dishonest receipt of $50 of negative taxes as more immoral than a taxpayer's taking a non-existent charity deduction that saved $50.

There are a number of technical problems that would have to be dealt with. For the computation of negative taxes, for example, income could not be "adjusted gross income" as defined for internal revenue purposes. The wealthy widow living on tax-exempt municipal bonds should not be eligible for negative payments. Probably those applying for negative taxes should be required to take the standard deduction, though perhaps exceptions should be made for certain catastrophic expenses. There is also the question of the taxable unit. Thomas K. Hitch suspects that many persons would set up their children as separate taxable units with zero incomes.[35] Then there is the matter of assets—what of the person with large non-income-yielding assets (such as idle land or cash under the mattress)? Or what of the movie actor whose income may be zero one year and many thousands the next? Some of these problems are unreal; others would require some thought and special regulations or requirements to keep the system from producing inequitable results. But they and others that are easy to conjure up make it clear that the system would be less simple than it might seem at first look.[36]

A more serious question has to do with the divorce of social services from cash payments. It is argued that counseling and other services providing intangibles to poor families can be more effectively done if the person supplying the services is the person who also supplies the cash to the family. The negative income tax would drive a wedge here; indeed, one of the arguments for it is that it would eliminate many or perhaps almost all of these services, and the paternalism that goes with them. This paternalism was discussed earlier, and the inference was plain that most of it could be dispensed with without adverse effect on the well-being

[35] "Why the Negative Income Tax Won't Work," *Challenge*, Vol. 14 (July–August 1966), p. 13.
[36] These questions are considered comprehensively in James Tobin, Joseph A. Pechman, and Peter M. Mieszkowski, "Is a Negative Income Tax Practical?" *Yale Law Journal*, Vol. 77 (November 1967), pp. 1–27 (Brookings Reprint 142). Their answer to their questioning title is affirmative.

of the community. But at most conceivable negative tax rates there would be some families who would need counseling and supplementary financial assistance. Finding and serving these people might be more difficult if the negative income tax were carrying the bulk of the burden, although presumably existing OEO programs could help to fill this need.[37]

For the sake of completeness, the list of problems includes the very real one of having to subsidize some of the nonpoor if incentives are to be preserved. Though this may not be important in substance, it does increase the political vulnerability of the plan. The nonpoor receiving subsidies would, of course, be near-poor.

The cost of a negative income tax would vary greatly, depending on the coverage, rates, and other features. Exact costing is not possible because it is not possible to predict just how people will react (in terms of work habits) to something as new as this, and because it is not known what the states would do with their assistance programs after negative income tax payments began.

Earlier in this chapter there was discussion of a proposal that paid 50 percent of the income deficit, the deficit to be calculated from the sum of the exemptions and the minimum standard deduction—$3,000 in the case of the family of four. This would put the guaranteed minimum at $1,500 for such a family. Lampman has estimated the cost of such a plan at about $8 billion in 1964, which would be offset by whatever reduction there was in public assistance. This might amount to $3 billion, which would make the net cost about $5 billion.[38] The cost would decline in each subsequent year, if the rates remained unchanged, as incomes rose.

A proposal by James Tobin suggests $400 per person for a family earning no income (a minimum of $1,600 for a family of four) coupled with a negative tax rate of one-third, which means that a family keeps two-thirds of each extra dollar earned, and that negative taxes are paid until income reaches $4,800 for the family of

[37] A recent report to the secretary of HEW by a group consisting largely of social workers has, however, recommended the separation of cash payments and the delivery of social services. American Public Welfare Association, *Public Welfare— Challenge to Validity* (APWA, Chicago, 1967).

[38] Robert J. Lampman, *Adding Guaranteed Income to the American System of Transfers* (University of Wisconsin, Institute for Research on Poverty, 1967), pp. 3–10. The study was prepared for OEO and was widely distributed by that agency.

four. He estimates the gross reduction in Treasury receipts to be $12 to $15 billion annually, again offset in part by reductions in public assistance payments.[39] Other programs would carry other price tags.[40]

Two features of "cost" are worth stressing. One is that in a basic sense there is no real cost attached to a negative income tax. While payers lose, recipients gain an equal amount. Thus, it uses up no resources, it has no impact on gross national product; in other words, it is quite unlike a Treasury expenditure for a squadron of bombers or a new highway. It would transfer resources from the private to the public sector and back to the private sector, or within the public sector, but it would not affect their size. The only modification of this generalization would occur if the negative income tax persuaded some people to stop working—the consequent loss of resources would be a real cost. But it is not at all clear that this would happen, particularly when it is thought of as a substitute for a system which clearly does destroy incentive (public assistance). If it resulted in more work rather than less— and it might do so—it would increase the total supply of goods and services, so that not only would there be no real costs but actually some positive real benefits.

Finally, over time the impact on the Treasury would change. If any system were instituted full-blown, the reduction in Treasury receipts would be greatest in the first year. In each following year, barring a recession, the amount of poverty would decline as the economy grew and as the poverty gap correspondingly declined. This is the same phenomenon that occurs on the positive side of the tax structure. Other things equal, the Treasury's receipts will grow each year as incomes and therefore tax yields grow.

It was pointed out earlier that it is highly unlikely that a negative income tax system would be instituted in comprehensive form all at once. Gradual introduction would not only be more likely but more sensible. If this is the case, it is important in costing to recognize that two offsetting factors will be at work: the growth of

[39] "The Case for an Income Guarantee," *The Public Interest* (Summer 1966), pp. 31–41.

[40] See Green, *Negative Taxes and the Poverty Problem*. This has a variety of negative income tax programs and estimated costs attached to each.

the coverage and amounts of payments as the law is enlarged and expanded, and the decrease in the number of recipients of negative tax payments as time passes and incomes grow.

The Family Assistance Plan

In the fall of 1969 a variation of the negative income tax, the Family Assistance Plan, proposed by President Nixon, was placed before the Congress. The major points of the bill as introduced correct some of the defects of the existing system but fail to correct others.[41] Briefly, the proposal included these elements:

1. Nearly all low-income families with children, including those headed by full-time workers, would be eligible to receive benefits. Only those with more than $1,500 in resources other than their homes, household goods, personal effects, and property essential to their livelihood, would be excluded.

2. The basic yearly federal payment for an eligible family would be at the rate of $500 a person for the first two family members plus $300 for each additional member. Thus there would be a federal income floor of $1,600 per year for a family of four with no other income.

3. If the family had other income, earned or unearned, of $720 or less per year, it would continue to receive the full basic federal payment. For other income in excess of $720 per year, the assistance benefits would be reduced $1 for each $2 of other income. For example, a family of four with earnings of $2,000 a year would receive a family assistance payment of $960, yielding a total income of $2,960. (The family is allowed to disregard $720 of its $2,000 earnings; of the remaining $1,280, 50 percent is deducted from the $1,600 basic federal payment, leaving a payment to the family of $960.) The break-even point—the level of income at which a family of four would cease to be eligible for any family assistance benefits—would be $3,920.

4. In order to receive benefits, adult members of the household would be required to register for work and to accept "suitable em-

41 H.R. 14173, 91 Cong. 1 sess.

ployment" when it was offered. Only the aged, the disabled, and mothers with children under six years of age would be relieved of this requirement.

5. Forty-two states in which benefit levels exceed the proposed federal minimum would be required to supplement federal benefits.

In some respects the Family Assistance Plan represents an almost revolutionary breakthrough in the area of welfare reform. For the first time there would be a national minimum benefit, although at less than half of the poverty line. In addition, the system would provide an incentive to work rather than not to work, and would provide no powerful motive for families to break up. Perhaps best of all, the old intrusive means test would be nearly abolished, and a new means test based on income would replace it.

While the plan would greatly improve matters in general, it does not go far enough in some areas and it goes the wrong direction in others.

1. The national minimum of $1,600 for a family of four, while far better than nothing, is still pitifully small. The wide disparity among benefit levels in the states would be somewhat narrowed by this minimum, but it would still be greater than two to one at the extremes.

2. By limiting the payments to families with children, the plan leaves out 20 percent of the population in poverty. The idea that people with children are more deserving than those without children rests on an obscure logic.

3. The requirement that people register for work and accept "suitable employment" when it is offered does violence to the principles of the negative income tax. The 50 percent tax rate should provide incentive enough for recipients to work. Requiring that they take jobs defined as "suitable" by someone else is tampering with market processes and, perhaps more importantly, imperiling the self-respect of the poor.

4. As under the present welfare system, recipients are prohibited from saving or owning assets of more than nominal value.

5. Although the federal plan calls for a marginal tax rate of 50 percent, the states will be permitted to reduce their supplemental benefits by 80 percent of earned income. This, when coupled with

social security and income taxes, will result in overall marginal rates of close to or over 100 percent in some states at some income levels, thus providing little or no work incentive. The basic difficulty here stems from the fact that the simple nationwide negative income tax outlined in this chapter would almost certainly have to be fully federal and administered by the Treasury Department. The President's proposal, on the other hand, retains the mixed HEW-state system of administration, with all of the inconsistencies and complexities inherent in such a system. It is not, nor will it be, a true negative income tax until its coverage is universal and it is fully integrated with the positive tax system.

In summary, then, the bill presents a great and important step toward welfare reform. It does not go all the way, however. In the interest of both equity and efficiency, the federal floor should be raised, extended to all who are needy, and made dependent solely on the recipient's income and not on his work habits.

There remains to consider how a negative income tax would fit into the war on poverty. Some think of it as doing the whole job, and in a formal sense it could do so; but this seems inappropriate. With or without a comprehensive income maintenance system, it is surely better both for society and for the poor to have employable members performing up to their potential; and the education, training, and other social programs are designed to assure this. So long as they are needed—and over time the need should decline—they should remain as measures to upgrade people and communities.[42]

There would be a substantial impact on other income maintenance programs. Public assistance would be largely or entirely replaced. If the negative income tax came gradually, the replacement would take place gradually and rather automatically. Public assistance payments would be defined by law either as income or not as income. In the former case states would be motivated to re-

[42] Perhaps the most complete picture of how a negative income tax would fit into the war on poverty generally is given in *Poverty Amid Plenty: The American Paradox.* This report of the President's Commission on Income Maintenance Programs contains an excellent discussion of present programs and recommends a negative income tax (with a $2,400 floor on income), and revisions in other programs to go along with it.

duce their payments and let the negative taxes take their place. In the latter case, states would supplement negative taxes until they became high enough to take over. In either case the state role would gradually wither away, so far as payments were concerned. States would no doubt experiment with the amount of nonfinancial services to be continued. There would also be a tax transfer effect from federal to state governments. The attractions of the negative income tax are many, and it is worthy of continued and careful study and experimentation. As a weapon in the war on poverty it could be highly important. If the nation were to decide that it really wanted to get rid of poverty, the negative income tax would surely be one of the most effective ways to do so. Combined with other opportunity-oriented programs, it will assure the elimination of poverty whenever the people decide they are ready to make the commitment.

CHAPTER VII

Evaluation, Planning, and Management

When the war on poverty was launched in late 1964 it carried with it an unusual attribute—a very real concern about "scientific" evaluation of its programs. Part of the new organization (staffed by economists, operations researchers, social scientists, systems analysts) was to keep score on the effectiveness of the several kinds of attack on poverty, and to help the director decide whether his resources were being used wisely or, more technically, "optimally." Evaluation would be a major input into planning, indicating which programs should be reduced, or increased, or eliminated in the move toward an optimal mix.

This notion had its roots in the experience of the Department of Defense, which had demonstrated the utility of such an approach in the years following the Kennedy inauguration. If benefit-cost analysis, five-year plans, and the rest of the newly developed kit of tools could help administrators choose rationally among alternative weapons systems, there seemed reason to try to adapt it to the war on poverty as well. Here too there would be competing alternatives that would require analysis and choice, and correct choices would minimize the use of resources to attain a given objective.

The OEO staff of analysts was recruited in the first months of 1965 and began work on evaluation, as well as the planning that is really an end product of evaluation. In line with the director's responsibilities for the entire poverty war, the concerns were not only for OEO's programs, though initial emphasis naturally went to these, but for plans encompassing the total federal effort.

In August 1965 the President, through the Bureau of the Budget, issued a directive requiring all federal agencies to establish staffs of this sort and to begin conducting analyses and submitting five-year plans. Gradually these have come into being. That for the war on poverty was the first (after the Department of Defense), leading other civilian agencies by about a year.

In a conceptual sense the evaluation of a poverty program is not difficult.[1] Its essence is the relation between the inputs and outputs, or costs and benefits. All programs have costs attached to them (they use up resources) and all have some benefits (which conceivably could turn out to be negative, but are normally positive). It is clear that the most desirable course is to achieve a given output or benefit for the least possible cost, or—what is logically equivalent—to achieve the largest possible output for a given cost. Sometimes this is referred to as cost-benefit; the desideratum is to maximize the difference between benefits and costs, or if ratios are used, to maximize the ratio of benefits to costs. When two programs are compared, the one with the larger difference or ratio is judged "better," using that adjective in this very precise sense.

Costs can be measured in terms of manpower used, or teacher time consumed, or time taken, but it is more customary to use dollars. Dollars are assumed to measure the use of resources rather well, and normally they do, though there are instances of temporary but significant shortages or bottlenecks that make money costs misleading, at least in the short run. On the benefit side, the analysis reverts to the definition of poverty, and benefits are counted in terms of movement of poor people across the poverty line. It would seem to follow then that of several programs, each costing $100 million, the one that takes the most people across the line is "best."

[1] The reader interested in more detail than will be presented here is referred to Robert Dorfman (ed.), *Measuring Benefits of Government Investments* (Brookings Institution, 1965), and Samuel B. Chase, Jr. (ed.), *Problems in Public Expenditure Analysis* (Brookings Institution, 1968).

Problems of Evaluation

But if the conceptualization of evaluation is straightforward enough, the actual implementation in the field of social welfare is enormously complex and difficult. Some of the problems are worth dwelling on briefly, if only to make clear that the state of the art is a long, long way from producing answers from a computer. Quantitative analysis can help make better decisions, but the major role remains that of human judgment.

In the poverty area one of the sticky problems derives from the inexact nature of the definition of the term. An output—perhaps the only output—of any specific poverty program should be the removal of people from poverty, and a program's effectiveness should be measured against this criterion. But it is not that simple. Is a program as effective when it moves a poor family from $3,000 per year to $3,200 as it is when moving one from zero to $3,200? Is it better to give a family $500 and thus move it above the poverty line or to spend $1,000 training its breadwinner so that his earning capacity can later be increased? It is quite easy to think of other examples of this sort of difficulty.

A closely allied problem is the frequent inability to quantify outputs of programs. A job-training program is designed to increase earnings, and the difference in earnings with and without training can be estimated and quantified. But there are almost always by-products as well—perhaps an increase in family stability, or a decrease in teen-age delinquency—to which quantities cannot be as easily attached. And how does one quantify whatever it is that money spent for free legal services to the poor is trying to do? In many instances it is possible to figure out ways to quantify, but analysis rarely succeeds in attaching quantities to the whole of the output. Handling the intangibles, the nonquantifiables, is what makes all this an art rather than a science.

There is, next, the matter of time. Most poverty programs are designed to have a lasting impact on their subjects. Head Start, for example, if successful will reduce the high school dropout rate nine to twelve years later, and will raise earnings of those in the program thirteen to sixty years later. But analysts work for impatient people who refuse to wait for a half century to see what the results are; resource allocation decisions have to be made now. So there is a search for proxies for the correct outputs, impacts which "reasonable people" will agree are closely related to these long-range effects. In Head Start, one examines the school record in first and second grades of those from similar backgrounds who have and have not had the Head Start experience; if those who had it perform significantly better than those who did not, there is a presumption that the program is beneficial (though not of course that it either is or is not worth its cost). There are dangers in the use of such proxies; if the initial benefits fade away after several years of schooling—and there is some evidence that they do —the proxy turns out to have been a misleading one.

There are, finally, never enough data of the right kind. The programs themselves generate a great many data, indicating the socioeconomic characteristics of the participants. But it takes time and great resources to gather this information, and frequently its accuracy is subject to question since it comes largely from applicants who are not used to answering such questions. It is even more difficult to keep track of participants after they leave the program, and their subsequent performance is the decisive information. Many who complete poverty programs have a way of just disappearing.

Another aspect of the data problem is that mere before-and-after information will not do. It is not appropriate to attribute differences only to the program in which people are involved. Other causes (not the least of which is the simple passage of time, especially for young people) may well have been at work, so that an "all other things equal" assumption is not warranted. What is needed is a control group, a group of people similar in all respects with the one exception that they were not in the program. It is frequently most difficult and sometimes quite impossible to find such a group. In Job Corps, for instance, a control group by definition would not have been in Job Corps; but the experts say that the fact that a young person did not apply, or did apply and was turned down, automatically makes him or her different and thus unsuitable for a control group.

These, and others that could be added, constitute a formidable set of difficulties. They have led some to the conclusion that benefit-cost analysis can only mislead, that it compels omission of the nonquantifiable which is frequently the most important aspect of either cost or benefit, or that the most important data are not available or obtainable. To deny this view is not to deny the difficulties. They exist, and they always will. But if rational allocation is important, it is necessary to undertake the sorts of comparisons that have been described. And the attempt leads to continual improvement of the decision-making process. In the struggle to understand the objectives of the rural loan program, for example, it became clear that if loans were going to young farmers the program was probably counterproductive, since it would tend to inhibit their movement to more productive occupations. This led to the urgency of collecting data on age of borrowers, and subsequently to the information that loans were not going to the young.

Similarly, in other programs, thinking formally about costs and about benefits frequently improves the ultimate judgment. At one time, with no output data at all, analysts determined the specific assumptions about the Neighborhood Youth Corps and Job Corps that would make them equally effective. The decision maker could then choose the set of assumptions that seemed more plausible to him; in this way it became possible to make a more rational choice between the programs. By quantifying part of the problem, by making assumptions explicit, by making the need for particular data apparent, officials find choices less difficult, though never easy.

Evaluation has many meanings. One might ask of a poverty program whether it is operating satisfactorily, that is, whether the staffing is excessive, whether the procedures are understood and consistent, and so on. This is a management-type evaluation, highly important in the sense that, if the program does not pass muster at this level, there is little point to looking into it further. But this is really only the beginning. Assuming that it is operating passably well, the next question is whether it is achieving its objectives. If it is an adult education program, is the curriculum such that adults do learn? If it is a job-training program, are skills being learned by the enrollees? Does money spent on family planning reduce the number of births unwanted by parents? In short, the point of interest is whether the programs are reaching the target groups for which they were designed and whether people in these groups are being affected in the appropriate manner.

Assuming affirmative answers to this set of questions, the next query is whether the achievement of objectives is contributing to the elimination of poverty, for this is the real payoff for such expenditures. On at least one occasion the director of OEO illustrated for a congressional committee the "success" of the adult literacy program by describing a seventy-five-year-old incapacitated man who learned to read and who, therefore, would be able to spend his few remaining months reading the Bible, which he had always wanted to do. Evaluation would point out in this case that the example showed that the program was successful in teaching adults to read, but the contribution to the elimination of poverty was essentially nil. Note the importance of the criterion selected in the evaluation process. If the criterion is "doing good" in some sense, the expenditure is hardly arguable; if it is elimination of poverty, the expenditure can only be regarded as wasteful.

Similar considerations relate to the ambiguity surrounding the relation between poverty and poor health and poor housing. Bad housing and bad health tend to be associated with poverty, but it is not completely clear that the relation is a causal one; at least the direction of the causal flow is not clear. If poverty is not caused by these things, then the best health or housing programs in the world, however meritorious in their own right, would be evaluated as inferior poverty programs.

The highest, and most difficult, level of evaluation is reached when one assumes that the objectives are being reached and that they are compatible with and contribute toward the elimination of poverty. The question then is whether any given program is the "best" way to do so. This is an extremely difficult question to answer, since it necessitates comparing things which, at least on the surface, are not comparable. Furthermore, the "best" poverty program is bound to be a mix of programs—not a single one—because the poverty population is so heterogeneous. There has been relatively little progress at this level of evaluation, except to sharpen intuitive judgments and to indicate the inevitability of choice and the importance of choosing as wisely as possible.

Examples of Evaluation

We turn now from the general to the specific, from the difference between conceptual straightforwardness and practical difficulties, to examine actual instances of evaluation of poverty programs. We shall see how halting the progress has been in terms of specific quantitative analyses, but it is well to keep in mind that one by-product of these attempts is a significant improvement in the staff's intuitive judgment about all programs.

FAMILY PLANNING

The relation between size of family and poverty has been observed many times. It is not only that the incidence of poverty is greater among large families; it is also more difficult for large families to exit from poverty. "Progress in reducing poverty in recent years is greatest among small-sized families, and is retarded to the extent that poor families continue to have high fertility rates."[2] The benefit-cost ratio for family planning should therefore be high, and this is the case, though just how high depends critically on the assumptions made about the effectiveness of the program.

The calculations are as follows. A five-year program is assumed for 1.5 million poor women of child-bearing age. Cost is set at $50 per year per woman, which is almost surely too high, but this is a common procedure since it will make the answer more plausible. That is to say, if the results look good in spite of a high cost figure, one feels even more comfortable with the result than he otherwise would.[3]

On the benefit side a very simple technique is used. Under the definition of poverty in Chapter 2 each member of the family adds a $500 requirement of income. Accordingly, each unborn member

[2] Harold L. Sheppard, *Effects of Family Planning on Poverty in the United States* (Upjohn Institute for Employment Research, 1967), p. 22.

[3] Among the practitioners, this is known as an *a fortiori* argument.

of a family may be regarded as "worth" $500. This is an annual worth for sixteen years,[4] but the annual flow of $500 must be discounted to obtain its present worth; at 5 percent this comes to $5,419 for each child whose birth is prevented.

The most difficult question is how to estimate the number of unborn children. This depends on how many women will use the family planning services faithfully, and how effective the services will be. It also involves the desires of the women participating. Poor people appear to want on the average no more children than the nonpoor have. Will this be what these women aim for, or will they, at the other extreme, simply stop bearing children at all when they find it possible to do so? Under uncertainty of this sort the practice is to make several different assumptions, trying to cover the range of possible outcomes, and see what the differences are.

In this case one extreme was the assumption that the program reached 50 percent of the women effectively—though program costs were sufficient to reach all—and that these women bore children henceforth at the same rate as nonpoor women. The other extreme was that the effective participation rate was 75 percent and that these women stopped having children after joining the program. These cases yield benefit-cost ratios respectively of 3.3 and 18.8. Both of these are very high and tend to confirm the notion that family planning is one of the most effective antipoverty programs. Benefit-cost ratios of this size are rare among government social programs.

JOB CORPS

A second program for which benefit-cost calculations have been made is Job Corps.[5] This experience will illustrate how inexact the method is and how carefully the assumptions must be scrutinized. The basic question here is whether the expenditure of

[4] Sixteen years is the basic minimum age for employment; Fair Labor Standards Act of 1938, as amended, 29 U.S.C. 201, et seq.

[5] The detailed description of method and results will be found in Glen G. Cain, *Benefit/Cost Estimates for Job Corps* (University of Wisconsin, Institute for Research on Poverty, 1967).

funds on exposing young men and women to the Job Corps experience is worthwhile. As always, the answer depends on a comparison of inputs and outputs, or costs and benefits. Let us see how it was done by Glen Cain in this case.

On the cost side Cain began with the money spent by the government on Job Corps, adjusted for the fact that in 1967 the average corpsman remained for five months. This included overhead expenses involved in running Job Corps and also the earnings foregone by the corpsman, the wages he would have earned if he had not been in the Job Corps. The value of the work performed by the corpsman while in training (such as cutting fire trails and planting young trees) was subtracted from the cost. This was also done for the transfer payments made to him and to his family, on the ground that these were not made in any direct connection with Job Corps; they could have been made if the enroller had never entered Job Corps. So calculated, the five-month cost for an enrollee was $3,500.

What about the benefits? The real question is what difference in earning capability results from the Job Corps experience. This will not be known for years, even decades. What is needed is a proxy, and in this case Cain found two, used them both, and found, fortunately, that they tended to give similar results. One proxy is based on educational achievement changes that take place in Job Corps. These are known quite accurately by before-and-after testing. There are fairly good data on the relation between level of education and expected lifetime earnings so that differences in expected earnings can be calculated and discounted to a present value.

A second proxy is based on a direct comparison of wages earned by ex-corpsmen with wages earned by comparable young people with no Job Corps experience, though the earlier warning about finding usable control groups should be kept in mind. The education proxy yielded a present value of from $3,600 to $5,900, the wage proxy $5,100. These yielded benefit-cost ratios ranging from 1.02 to 1.70. Cain calculated other ratios based on different assumptions, but concluded that the interval cited here encompassed "a set of ratios that are conservative and realistic."[6]

[6] *Ibid.*, p. 5.

It could be argued that, with all the uncertainties and errors attached to this calculation, the ratios, at least at the low end, are not really enough above unity to be significant or meaningful. This is perhaps the case, but this is a very good example of the importance of the nonquantifiable elements, and of the importance too of the role of judgment in combination with benefit-cost analysis. In the family planning case the ratios were so high as to indicate clearly that the program was "good" and should be expanded. In Job Corps, this is not quite the case; what ratios of this size should indicate is the need to look very closely at elements that did not enter the calculation.

What are some of these? Some could be quantified but have not been. Higher earnings are associated with lower crime rates, lower welfare costs, higher tax payments. All of these effects would push up the ratios if they had been included. Also, there are some benefits that can never be quantified. Higher earnings go with greater family stability, a better functioning democracy, and other social effects that most people think of as good. Are there costs that have not entered the ratio? One might be the tendency of Job Corps centers to disrupt communities in which they are located. But "intuition tell us" that these intangible costs are much smaller than the intangible benefits. So the decision maker comes to the conclusion that if the benefit-cost ratio is near one without all these other benefits, the program is clearly worthwhile.

One other program hint comes from these calculations. Since a good share of Job Corps cost per corpsman is fixed, it becomes clear that extending the average length of stay is a very effective way to push up the benefit-cost ratio. This has suggested to Job Corps administrators that particular attention should be given to ways to extend the corpsmen's tenure.

Evaluation and planning are only part of the decision-making process, however, and while the foregoing analysis indicates that Job Corps is a program of some value, OEO has faced almost continuous criticism of the program and its operation. Community relations, seemingly high cost figures, and questions about the value of the output from the program have all contributed, both through public opinion in general and congressional action, to making the Job Corps one of OEO's major worries.

We have seen that Job Corps has not been an inexpensive venture, with costs of about $3,500 for the average five-month stint. The question is whether costs of this magnitude should be regarded as excessive. Some spurious analogies have been brought forward to make them look too large—for instance, "Harvard educates a boy for less," or "the public school per student costs are only around $700." These are not relevant. Job Corps enrollees are people who have failed in everything so far; they come from the most disadvantaged backgrounds. To turn them around is not easy and it is not cheap. It is necessary to work with them not six or eight hours a day, but twenty-four; not five days a week, but seven. Staff ratios and costs are correspondingly high—no doubt higher than expected—which is one reason why fewer young men and women have been taken than was originally contemplated. Seen in this light, $3,500 becomes understandable. To answer the question whether it is too high, one must know what it is buying. As shown above, the results seem to justify expenditures of this magnitude, but the figure still sounds high, and the criticism was probably instrumental in the Nixon administration's decision to close down the more expensive rural centers and replace them with urban minicenters.[7] Whether the consequent lowering of unit costs will cause a relative rise or fall in benefit-cost ratios remains to be seen.

LOAN PROGRAMS

Other examples where quantification has been pushed this far are not available, though in due course they no doubt will be. But in a number of other programs the analytical framework has been useful in improving the yield of antipoverty expenditures. One such case involves the Small Business Development Centers which were created by the Economic Opportunity Act. The plan, as was described in Chapter 3, was to help poor people, mostly but not entirely in urban areas, by extending low-interest loans to make possible the beginning of new businesses or the expansion of existing ones. The evaluation of the program disclosed that, although low-interest loans were being extended, they were not being ex-

[7] The program called for closing 59 of the existing 113 Job Corps centers and opening 30 small, intercity and near-city training centers, with a resultant drop in Job Corps training capacity of about one-third. *New York Times*, April 12, 1969.

tended to poor people, who generally are not very well suited to this particular type of improvement in their condition, and the loans made for little increase in the number of poor people employed. Thus cost-benefit analysis, which requires that the desired benefit be precisely defined, revealed that although the program served laudable ends, the direct elimination of poverty was not one of them. For this as well as other reasons it was dropped by OEO.

A somewhat similar case was the rural loan program. The contribution to the elimination of poverty would be negative—not merely zero—if it had the effect of holding in marginal farming people who in the long run would be better advised to seek more productive employment. One of the first questions asked about the program, therefore, was what sorts of people were receiving the loans. The data indicated that 50 percent of the loans were going to those over forty-five-years of age.[8] Since there is a presumption that these older people will not change occupations in any case, at the very least it follows that the program is not producing negative benefits. This is not to say, of course, that a rural loan program is the best or even a good way to attack rural poverty.

HEAD START

Evaluation of Head Start has produced some interesting results. Formal benefit-cost ratios have not been computed, but many analyses of the impact on school performance have been made. One reason why truly definitive results have not been forthcoming has been the difficulty of finding adequate control groups because of the sheer size of the numbers enrolled. It is difficult to find poor youngsters who have not attended a summer Head Start program who are not also distinguished by other than random factors from those who have attended one.

This is a program, too, in which many benefits are of the non-quantifiable kind. Supposedly a preschool educational program only, it really has many other facets: for example, there is a conscious effort to make an impression on the family in the home as well as the child in the school; and there is a major diagnostic and reme-

---

[8] U.S. Office of Economic Opportunity, *The Tide of Progress* (1968), p. 82.

dial aspect—almost all children are given medical and dental examinations, many for the first time in their lives.

Head Start evaluation has concentrated on determining the changes in educational capability resulting from a program of six or eight weeks in the summer before school starts. The research that has been performed leaves little doubt that the cognitive abilities of those who have the experience are increased more than they would have increased without the experience. Research also shows, however, that those who have not had summer Head Start tend to catch up during the first year or two of schooling to those who did. The data on both these findings are a little ambiguous, and the lack of adequate control groups weakens the precision of the findings, but the broad conclusions are no doubt valid.

Two program changes have come from these findings. One is a growing emphasis on full-year Head Start, in the hope that the longer experience will produce more lasting effects. The second is a Follow Through program designed to work for a year or more with the most needy summer Head Start "graduates" to try to preserve and extend the benefits. It is still too early to know what success either of these additions is achieving.[9] It might be noted at this point that the chances of real success of these programs are no doubt quite remote unless a number of other measures go forward simultaneously. These include a truly basic improvement in the educational system in disadvantaged areas, particularly the urban ghettos, an order-of-magnitude change in housing, and greater stability and cohesiveness of the family. Most important, all of these are needed simultaneously or slum area youngsters are most unlikely to retain through twelve years of perfunctory schooling the advantages they obtain from Head Start at age five or six.

COMMUNITY ACTION PROGRAM

Finally, there is the very special problem of how to evaluate the community action program. This is special simply because it is so

---

[9] A Westinghouse Learning Corporation evaluation suggests that success is still an elusive goal in Head Start. *The Impact of Head Start: An Evaluation of the Effects of Head Start on Children's Cognitive and Affective Development* (Ohio University Press, 1969).

difficult. There are some components of CAP that are neither more nor less difficult to evaluate than other programs—Head Start, Upward Bound, legal services, for instance. But community action as a comprehensive, innovative set of programs is intended to be something more than the sum of its components.

The peculiar difficulty of CAP evaluation rests on the inability to specify the objectives unambiguously. What is it that CAP is really trying to do? It is presumably some combination of institution changing and income raising. The first is almost impossible to specify with any precision, let alone measure.[10] The second is measurable enough, but attributing causation can be very treacherous; furthermore, CAP deals with target areas, in which by no means all are poor according to the official definition.

In recognition of these problems, eight comprehensive CAP evaluation studies were begun in the summer of 1966. Contracts were let to universities or research organizations in six metropolitan areas and two rural areas in which CAPs were operating. The tasks of the contractors were not rigidly specified. In each case a mixed team of social scientists was told to study its particular area in great detail and to see what happened to numerous variables—income, employment, divorce, delinquency—and to attribute causation where possible. Furthermore, the groups were to suggest, on the basis of their experience, different methodologies for overcoming the difficulties inherent in evaluating a program such as CAP. The groups were left to operate independently of each other, so that significance could be attached where there was substantial agreement or disagreement among them on methodology.

By October 1969 all of the reports had been completed or were near completion. While some time must elapse before the large mass of material that was collected can be sorted out and systematically analyzed, a number of general conclusions about CAP evaluation have already been reached.

The greatest problem with evaluating CAP, according to the reports, stems from the fact that in no case has the program had

[10] However, the study mentioned in Chap. 4 has some interesting and positive things to say about this. Barss, Reitzel and Associates, *Community Action and Institutional Change,* An Evaluation Prepared for the Office of Economic Opportunity (Cambridge, Mass.: Barss, Reitzel, 1969).

nearly enough money to achieve a significant fiscal impact on the area's poor. While in almost all cases the evaluators were able to collect significant types of heretofore unavailable data and to make before-and-after comparisons about the lot of persons in the target group, it was generally extremely difficult to isolate the impact of CAP from the impact of economic growth and other programs. With regard to the sociological and institution-changing results, it was easier to separate the influence of CAP. As might have been expected, the effectiveness of the program in these fields appeared to have varied widely among the CAPs studied.

Other efforts to evaluate CAP are less imaginative. A number of community action agencies have been examined in depth. In some cities jobs are being found, in some the employment service is being reoriented toward the poor, in some public housing rules have been improved, and so on. But the impression one gets is that changes in other programs—for example, public assistance—tend to overwhelm in effect anything that CAP is doing. This is a natural consequence of the fact that nowhere is CAP large enough to be a significant social factor. Since there is no city where CAP is an investment as large as 5 percent of the city's welfare budget, this is hardly surprising.

Because of inadequate funding plus the decision of OEO to spread CAP thinly over the country, there is no way to determine whether a generously funded program would have the beneficial impact it is designed to have. This is very unfortunate since information should be accumulated, during the lean days when the total impact on poverty is minimal, to determine which programs have real promise of achievement when and if the resources finally become available.

These are a few examples of the way evaluation has played a role in the war on poverty. In some cases actual benefit-cost ratios were computed, though in no case could all benefits and all costs be included. In other cases this was quite out of the question, given the present state of the art; even then the framework is useful, and the attempt to think rigorously about what appropriate benefits are in any one case often leads to program modifications that are clearly in the direction of better resource allocation.

Planning

We next examine how evaluation leads into the planning process. The appraisals of the poverty programs should furnish a basis for recommending the "best" programs for each target group, and thus for putting together the "best" package for an overall plan. This package, with costs attached to each component for each of the next five years, becomes what is called the program budget which, under the federal planning-programming-budgeting (PPBS) system, is to be submitted to the Bureau of the Budget each year. After it is accepted by the bureau, perhaps with modifications of its own, the budget for the first year of the five becomes the budget that is submitted to the Congress for the next fiscal year.

The discussion earlier should have made clear that hard and fast decisions on what is best are not possible in the present state of the art. Instead, a mixture of hard evaluation and intuitive judgment, based on a growing understanding of the programs as experience is gained, is brought to bear on the process of selecting programs for inclusion in the plan.

These programs are matched to the several target groups in poverty; here the information can be quite precise, at least for the present or near-term future. Figures are available on the numbers of poor children and old people, and on the amount of rural poverty. Estimates can be made of how these figures will change in future years; this in turn will depend in part on the extent and effect of the poverty programs in intervening years. At the beginning of the planning process no financial constraints are imposed; the fundamental question asked is, given so many poor people of certain characteristics, what will it take to get them out of poverty and how long will it take? Other constraints are recognized, however: housing programs can be instituted only as quickly as supply bottlenecks can be broken, and health programs must wait for doctors and nurses to be trained and ways found to coax them into poverty areas.

In a comprehensive plan of this sort, the various parts reinforce each other. Thus, it is important that the income maintenance portions should not have incentive penalties, particularly for those eligible for manpower training or ready for employment. There needs to be recognition of the fact that some parts of the poverty population cannot benefit from manpower policy; others clearly can. This means that, as those whose principal hope of economic well-being lies in the labor market are trained and placed, the incentive aspects of income maintenance become less important. The process of making the various segments of the plan consistent with each other is complex.

The absence of financial constraints in the initial construction of the plan assures that the cost of the first plan will be high—probably a substantial multiple of the budget of the year preceding the first year of the plan. On the assumption that the President will not feel able to commit so much money, the next feature is an ordering process, which shows a series of decreasingly expensive plans, and which seeks to assure that, whatever the resource commitment ultimately decided on, the plan available would be the "best" plan, in the sense that it would buy more poverty elimination than any other combination of programs costing the same amount.

The first comprehensive plan for the war on poverty was drawn up in 1966, for the five-year period from July 1, 1967, to June 30, 1972. Estimates indicated that the adoption of this plan would reduce the number of poor by 1972 to 10.9 million (that is, the number below the current poverty income lines, corrected for price changes). In addition, while detailed costing and programming beyond 1972 was not done, it nevertheless became clear that it was within reach to reduce the number of 10.9 million to zero by 1976 without exorbitant expenditures of funds.

This was the source for the statement of Sargent Shriver, OEO director, to the Senate Committee on Labor and Public Welfare that poverty could be eliminated in ten years, or by the two hundredth anniversary of the signing of the Declaration of Independence.[11] The committee scarcely noticed the comment, and the press generally reacted with skepticism.

[11] *Amendments to the Economic Opportunity Act of 1964,* Hearings before the Subcommittee on Employment, Manpower, and Poverty of the Senate Committee on Labor and Public Welfare, 89 Cong. 2 sess. (1966), p. 53.

Actually, that an investment of resources well within the nation's capability could have accomplished such a goal was apparent to any careful student of the problem. The total poverty gap in 1966 was only $12 billion and would decline in each subsequent year. The plan contemplated moving most people out of poverty through training and education and, in the later years when most of the remaining poor were not able to move into the labor market, relying on a comprehensive income maintenance program to take over and raise the remaining families above the poverty lines. Costs of such a program have never been announced, but they were well within the nation's capabilities, far less than one year's growth in disposable income.

Policy Effects

There remains to ask about the impact on policy of planning and evaluation. So far as comprehensive planning is concerned the impact has been minimal or nil. The plans have specified several levels of expenditures, called something like "adequate" at the most generous to "minimal" at the least generous. The actual budget approved by the President—for fiscal 1967 and later years—has been a small fraction of the lowest level suggested by the plan. If the plans suggested possible levels of $10, $8, and $6 billion for the war on poverty, the President approved $2 billion, and the Congress then reduced that. Whether Vietnam expenditures or something else was the cause, it is clear that the plans had virtually no impact on policy, since at the low level approved the planners had not attempted any optimization.

If the plans had little or no impact, what about program evaluation? Here again the impact was blunted. Much more important than effectiveness was popularity. For example, Head Start has been popular both in the White House and in Congress; it is a matter of speculation what will happen now that evaluation has indicated that Head Start may be ineffective. Similarly, Neighborhood Youth Corps, whose effectiveness from the start seemed questionable, was popular and Congress always added funds to those asked by the agency. Contrariwise, the analysts felt that local option community action funds should be increased so that experience with local programs and initiative could be gained, but this part of community action was unpopular and was progressively reduced for several years.

One should not infer from all this that analysis had no impact or is not worth doing. After all, politics will always play a role in anything as controversial as the war on poverty, and it should. Furthermore, hard evaluation results are not yet available for a single program; there is no program that can be rigorously proven to be bad or good. Finally, as has been indicated, there have been some policy impacts. There is experimentation with longer Head Starts; the work experience program has been phased out and a Work Incentive program instituted; Job Corps has been kept from growing and its form basically changed; manpower has been made more central to the whole effort. All of these things, and more, resulted from analyses that indicated how resources should be reallocated.

Even if planning has thus far had little impact, evaluation has had some effect. And it has had it even though it is still imperfectly used and quite incomplete. But working at it has made many program aspects clearer than they would otherwise have been, and hence has helped administrators to make better choices. Analysts are not making the decisions, nor should they; the most they can hope to do is to supply an input that will help the decision maker. This they have been doing, and with increasing authority.

Program Management and Coordination

The original act authorized the director of OEO to call on any other federal agency for information and "other materials," directed other agencies to cooperate with the director and to carry out their programs so as to assist in achieving the aims of the Economic Opportunity Act, and instructed the director to assist the President in coordinating the antipoverty efforts of all federal agencies.

This was a sweeping and rather unusual statutory instruction, and it is necessary to observe how it has worked. The task of the director was greatly complicated by the variety of his original assignments. Part of what he was coordinating were operating programs run by him: VISTA, Job Corps, and the community action program. He delegated others, including Neighborhood Youth Corps, which in some respects was a competitor of Job Corps. Finally, he had to be interested in many others, and some of these were potential competitors with programs that he ran or delegated—for example, model cities and community action overlapped in many respects. Thus the director was both operator and coordinator; he was both competitor and coordinator in the federal bureaucracy, and this did not ease his varied duties. In addition, there was pressure from the very beginning to "get OEO out of the operating business" so that it could do a more effective job of coordinating. There are two sides to this, but there is little doubt that the operating responsibilities made the coordinating function more difficult.

On the formal level, the coordination was to be effected through the Economic Opportunity Council, a cabinet level committee under the chairmanship of the OEO director. At the first meeting of this council, at which the President was present, the hope was expressed that the council would become the "domestic security council" of the war on poverty.[12] This was a hope that was never realized; indeed, the council had very limited usefulness as an instrument of coordination.

The reason for this failure is not difficult to find. The National Security Council is presided over by the President, who is able to make decisions. His is the authoritative voice and all present recognize it as such. In the Economic Opportunity Council, on the other hand, the chairman was outranked by most of the other members, who were cabinet members. An attempt was made to compensate for this by having the Vice President attend the meetings as honorary chairman. He attended faithfully and lent great support to the chairman, but even this did not permit the chairman to make his views prevail whenever any other member disagreed. All this was not helped any during the period when the relations between President Johnson and the Kennedys were casting

<hr/>

[12] *New York Times,* Nov. 12, 1965.

a cloud over the President's confidence in and sympathy for Sargent Shriver—a Kennedy in-law.

As a consequence, the discussions at the council tended to become information exchanges, a not unimportant function but hardly coordination. After the first two or three meetings the principals began to send lower-ranking substitutes, a sure sign in Washington that nothing important is going to happen.

Under the 1967 amendments, the makeup and functions of the Economic Opportunity Council were revised. As before, the director and the heads of relevant agencies and departments sat on the council, but the director, although he continued to hold a special position in the war on poverty, was no longer automatically the chairman.[13] The amendments provided for an executive secretary of the council, appointed by the President and not directly associated with OEO. It is the declared purpose of the council to coordinate programs, develop policies, set priorities, resolve differences among federal departments, and even initiate projects consonant with the purposes of the Economic Opportunity Act. Within the legislative history and intent of these provisions was the idea that the executive secretary could become a figure of cabinet rank and that the council could, accordingly, develop real power in functioning as a general coordinator of the war on poverty. Two years later, this had yet to happen, but the amendments provided a potential which before had not existed even on paper. However, the Urban Affairs Council of the Nixon administration, located in the White House and associated with the name of Daniel P. Moynihan, in its first few months acted to fill many of the functions that were envisaged for the Economic Opportunity Council.

At the informal level much more coordination was accomplished. OEO created the Office of Interagency Relations (later the Office of Governmental Relations) which worked with other agencies either on specific problems as they materialized or on ways to improve the coordination process. In developing plans for the war on poverty there has been constant communication among all agencies. Specific situations called for special arrangements, as

---

[13] The statute now provides (Section 631(a)) that "the President shall designate one of the members of the Council to serve as chairman."

when in 1966 the agencies involved in manpower programs created a series of interagency teams to work in cities on coordination.[14] Some of these ventures seem to have been successful, others may not have been; coordination is not easy to achieve, but it is something to which OEO has paid much attention.

Program Delegation

A special case of coordination—the delegation of programs—merits attention. Of the programs outlined earlier, only community action and VISTA are now actually operated by OEO; the others are delegated to Labor, HEW, Agriculture, or other agencies. For a delegated program the authorization is normally written into the Economic Opportunity Act, the appropriation for the program is made to OEO, and the funds and authority are delegated by OEO's director to the other agency, which then operates the program. The statute usually does not provide that a program must be delegated, nor does it select the delegate agency. Delegations, however, are agreed to by the Congress and the executive branch, at least in the normal case, so that there are no surprises. If a delegation were changed, it would be almost certainly with the approval of the President and with the concurrence of the appropriate congressional committees. Delegation is not something lightly done or changed. Although the director officially does the delegating, the authority is in most cases his in a legal sense only, not in a real sense.

The business of delegating has raised a number of questions. Not the least of these is who is responsible for a delegated program. It might seem clear that OEO's director should be responsible—it is his authorization by law and the funds are his by appropriation. But it is not that simple. While the director has to fit the delegated programs into the overall war against poverty, each agency administering a delegated program also has its own constit-

[14] Sar A. Levitan, *The Great Society's Poor Law: A New Approach to Poverty* (Johns Hopkins Press, 1969), p. 57; and *Manpower Report of the President, 1967*, p. 68.

uency to think of, and conflicts have never been far below the surface.

Two examples may particularize this potential or actual conflict. OEO always felt it needed up-to-date information about "its" programs, and early set about instituting reporting procedures for the delegated as well as the in-house programs. It was well over a year before OEO finally prevailed on the Office of Education to impose on the states the simplest reporting system for the adult literacy program. Even then the reports contained detail that OEO regarded as unsuitable. The Office of Education argued that more detailed requirements would alienate the states, and this it was fearful of doing. Indeed, it seemed unwilling even to ask those states which refused to submit the required reports to do so. Quite clearly the office was concerned about its continuing relations with the states. OEO, on the other hand, was concerned to know who the people were who were being trained by "its" program and with "its" funds and continually pressed for a tougher federal attitude, as well as for changes in the way the program was being conducted. This conflict was never resolved, and by the time the program was taken out of the Economic Opportunity Act and given to the Office of Education, OEO was convinced that it did not really matter. With weak leadership of the program in Washington and the requirement to work through the states, an adult literacy program that would significantly help the poor seemed unattainable. In this case OEO felt that delegation made an effective program impossible.

Neighborhood Youth Corps is a second illustration of the difficulties stemming from delegation. Here the question revolved about how the available NYC funds should be spent. OEO felt that the purposes of the war on poverty would best be served if the out-of-school youth in NYC were given some education and some concentrated counseling. Otherwise, OEO urged, the youngsters were just being kept off the streets for a period of time on what frequently seemed like make-work projects, and the remedial aspects were lacking. The Department of Labor, on the other hand, was under great pressure to enroll as many NYC youngsters as possible; the program was very popular in Congress, largely because it did keep the young people off the streets. The education and counseling—"enrichment" it came to be called—would have added more than 20 percent to the cost of each enrollee, permitting only about 80 percent as many enrollees. OEO preferred 80 percent enriched; the Labor Department felt it important to maximize the number of enrollees, which meant no enrichment.

Whose program was it? Who made such policy decisions? The director could direct, but the department secretary decided whether to comply. In this case he did not comply; the only way to force him was to take the issue to the White House, probably to the President when both parties felt so strongly. This was not done, and for many months the program was operated at variance with the considered judgment of the President's chief of staff about how "his" funds ought to be spent. Why did the director not cut off the funds? To ask such a question is to answer it. The issue was not that important, and also neither the Bureau of the Budget nor the White House staff would have permitted such a family squabble to develop.

The issue was temporarily resolved in 1966 when the amendments to the act required a portion of the funds to be used for enrichment; but the appropriation that went with this action was a larger portion of the total than OEO liked. So in a sense OEO got its enrichment but had to pay for it. The lesson is, it would seem, that once a program is delegated, a large part of the policy determination goes with it.

Yet the purpose of OEO is to win the war on poverty, not simply to administer directly as many relevant programs as it can get its hands on. Although in certain areas, notably the ones just discussed, it can be plausibly argued that greater OEO supervision would have better served the needs of the poor, this is not to say that delegation is on balance a bad thing. For while it is true almost by definition that in delegating or transferring a program OEO loses a good deal of control, control is not the prime issue. The question is whether, in delegating a program, the quantity and/or quality of services to the poor stand to be improved. In order to ensure that the interests of the poor are taken into account by the administering agency, however, it is desirable that OEO be well informed on what is being done in the field. In this situation

OEO can both serve its special function as lobbyist for the poor in Washington and facilitate the employment of the considerable funds, knowledge, and other resources of the administering agency. One case in which this was done, albeit with certain difficulties, was in the delegation to the Department of Labor of OEO's locally oriented manpower programs.

After the passage of the 1966 Economic Opportunity amendments, the Economic Opportunity Act provided for a number of manpower programs for the poor. NYC was already administered by the Department of Labor. The Special Impact and New Careers programs were as yet not in operation. The Green Thumb program, administered by OEO, was in limited operation in some localities.[15] Furthermore, a CAP manpower division was operating local programs on its own. Thus in the fall of 1966 there was provision for five separate local manpower programs, scattered throughout the act under different sections and titles, some with specifically earmarked appropriations, some without.

OEO was faced with two alternatives. Either the new programs could be given to CAP, to be administered by the CAAs in conjunction with the already extant CAP manpower division, or they could be delegated to the Department of Labor. The group at OEO that finally won out argued strongly for delegation to Labor, for a number of reasons. It was felt that Labor's manpower staff would be better able to run the programs coherently than would CAP, which had only three professionals in its manpower division at that time. It was also felt, in light of Labor's recently professed interest in reaching the poor more effectively, that if the new programs could be integrated with the better features of existing Labor programs, both agencies, and most importantly the poor, would benefit. On the other hand, delegation would be acceptable to OEO only if the CAA were made the focus of the local manpower programs, for it was "the guiding principle of OEO that the local CAA must be the focal point of anti-poverty activity if the Agency is to be successful in reaching the poor."[16] Thus, if delega-

---

[15] For a description of the three programs, see Chap. 5.

[16] Robert A. Levine and Walter Williams, "Effective Administration of Manpower Programs for the Poor" (internal document, Office of Economic Opportunity, April 14, 1967), p. 6.

tion could be accomplished in such a way as to include the CAA on the local level, manpower, one of the basic foundations of a successful poverty program, would be combined with community action, the heart of the war on poverty, while the administrative coherence provided by having all the programs under one roof in Washington would make for increased flexibility in planning and funding.

This mix was first tried in the field in the spring of 1967 under what was called the Concentrated Employment Program. Although CEP still operates as a program in its own right and has now become a model for the proposed comprehensive Manpower Training Act, it has also served to some extent as a pilot project for the OEO-Labor delegation agreements. The purpose of CEP is to provide comprehensive and systematic manpower services for the poor in the country's worst poverty-unemployment areas. To this end the CAA in each CEP target area has access to any and all of the manpower programs which might be called for by a given situation. The CAA and the local public Employment Service work together to provide a complete range of counseling, training, and placement services. Thus, whereas in non-CEP areas there is a New Careers project, or NYC, or some other, a CEP target area will have all of these programs available to its residents. In 1967 CEP used the appropriations for the New Careers and Special Impact projects, some NYC money (NYC was already operated by Labor), and some Green Thumb money. Since all of these, while remaining intact within the Department of Labor as individual programs, were administered as component parts of a comprehensive program, the individual needs of each CEP target area could be handled with considerable flexibility. In drawing together the resources of OEO, community action, the Department of Labor, and the Employment Service, CEP, although beset by the problems facing any new and sophisticated program at its outset, showed enough promise in its early months for the Senate Committee on Labor and Public Welfare to term it "altogether ... potentially the best coordinated manpower effort developed so far."[17] The committee went on to recommend, as both OEO and Labor

[17] *Economic Opportunity Amendments of 1967*, S. Rept. 563, 90 Cong. 1 sess. (1967), p. 25.

had recommended, that the 1967 amendments place all of the locally oriented manpower programs together under a new Title I-B (Work and Training for Youth and Adults), so that the flexibility achieved by CEP could be extended to all manpower efforts directed at the poor. This was done and, as was the legislative intent, the combination of programs was delegated to the Department of Labor. The omnibus provision, by putting all the programs in one place and by removing the upper age limit on out-of-school NYC, provided a continuous range of manpower training services for the poor.

At the same time CEP was encouraging direct federal-local relations, the Department of Labor (after consulting with HEW and OEO) began to develop the Cooperative Area Manpower Planning System (CAMPS) to encourage coherent planning on all levels. Originally designed as an informal agreement to communicate and cooperate, CAMPS became an instrument of governmental policy in August 1968, when the President made it the subject of an executive order. The CAMPS structure of local, state, regional, and national committees was regarded as appropriate to the local nature of manpower programs, and was considered the primary instrument for carrying out the policy of cooperative planning and coordination of manpower programs. CAMPS was intended to minimize confusion and duplication of programs—a purpose that would be enhanced by the Nixon administration's proposed comprehensive Manpower Training Act, which would give communities the option of retaining CAMPS or setting up similar structures.[18]

OEO did not at first give up all of its control over Title I-B projects. A Memorandum of Agreement of April 1968 between OEO and Labor specified the division of labor and authority between the two agencies. The memorandum made explicit that the CAA was the presumptive prime sponsor for any of the projects, and provided that the presumption could be rebutted only with OEO's agreement; in other words, the CAA would administer any program unless it agreed not to. Furthermore, OEO and the CAAs retained responsibility for establishing eligibility requirements

<hr>

[18] See *Manpower Report of the President*, January 1969, pp. 129–31, and Sar A. Levitan and Garth L. Mangum, *Federal Training and Work Programs in the Sixties* (Ann Arbor, Mich.: Institute of Labor and Industrial Relations, 1969), pp. 424–27.

and for ensuring that the programs employed poor people where possible. At the top, the director exercised planning, programming, and budgetary control functions, and had to be consulted about any major policy changes that Labor chose to make. It is probable, however, that OEO had less power in fact than it did on paper, as program definition, in the last analysis, takes place in the field, where Labor was and is administrative king.[19] The comprehensive Manpower Training Act proposed by President Nixon in August 1969, which was mentioned in Chapter 5, if adopted, would transfer jurisdiction over Title I-B entirely to the Department of Labor. Since these programs have shown considerable promise, this is not surprising, and is in line with the administration's general policy of using OEO as an experimental and planning agency rather than an administrative one.

The delegation of the I-B programs to the Department of Labor had a significant impact upon that department. It provided considerable impetus to a general reorganization and reorientation of the department, which has become more explicitly concerned with the problems of poverty. In 1969 Labor experienced an administrative shuffling which created within the Manpower Administration the U.S. Training and Employment Service (USTES), an amalgam administering the functions of the former Bureau of Employment Security, except those relating to unemployment insurance, and all manpower training programs, including those under Title I-B. USTES is heavily oriented toward antipoverty work. The Job Opportunities in the Business Sector program (JOBS) furnishes training for the poor and helps provide positions for them. The future position of the CAA in coordinating manpower programs is not yet clear. The Department of Labor has ordered that all CAAs use the local Employment Services to provide manpower services. Just how much this requirement will weaken the CAA's manpower initiative remains to be seen.

It is implicit in the meaning of delegation that the delegating agency loses a considerable amount of control over its programs. This has been the case with Title I-B, and in fact the delegation is likely to result in complete transfer of the programs to the Labor

---

[19] "Delegation Memorandum of Agreement" (internal document, Office of Economic Opportunity, April 12, 1968).

Department. Yet, as has been emphasized, the purpose of OEO is to get at the problem of poverty in America. It cannot be disputed that the changes in the organization and perceived purposes of the Department of Labor act toward this end. There are now more and better manpower programs directed at the poor than was the case three years, or even one year, ago. Providing better services for the poor and making other agencies more aware of their problems and thus better able to deal with them are major parts of OEO's job; if the best way to realize these ends is delegation, or even transfer, it is OEO's job to delegate or transfer.

Through all of this the role of the Office of Economic Opportunity as manager of the war on poverty has been ambiguous and controversial. For the first four years it tried to serve as both operator and coordinator. It ran the Job Corps and VISTA and the highly visible community action program. Included under community action were programs like legal services and Head Start which were, as far as the statute was concerned, part of community action but in fact stood on their own feet.

The coordination function met with only mediocre success. Questions of when to delegate and whether and when to transfer programs were never easily answered, and usually became caught up in bureaucratic disputes. The agency did serve as a spokesman for the poor within the executive branch, but it never developed its influence sufficiently to have a serious impact on the course of the war on poverty.

With the coming into power of the new administration in early 1969, it was natural that substantial changes would take place. An early message from the President to the Congress indicated that he did not want the agency to die. This was followed by a number of months of speculation about just what would happen, followed on August 11 by an announcement from the President that he was reorganizing the OEO. It was difficult to estimate what the impact of this reorganization would be. It did confirm, however, that the operating function was to be downgraded and that the policy of transferring programs as they developed was made even more firm. OEO retained VISTA, legal services, some neighborhood health services, and community action. Its prime charge appeared to be experimenting with new ways of alleviating poverty, and its director apparently was to retain an influential voice in the executive branch of government as far as poverty programs were concerned. The agency itself was expected to put great emphasis on research and evaluation, along with experimentation. It appeared that there would be less delegation in the future and more rapid transfer of programs that seemed to work. What impact this reorganization would have on the war on poverty remained to be seen. There was no indication that substantial additional resources would be made available, and without these the likelihood of a genuine impact was as small as before.

CHAPTER VIII

Assessment

There remains the summing up. Is it all sound and fury, or is there some substance to it? Has anyone moved out of poverty who would not have anyway? Given the fact that any kind of federal expenditure will generate new income and that some of this usually reaches the low-income population, have antipoverty expenditures had an impact above and beyond that resulting from the simple expenditure of funds? These are not easy questions to answer, and the very fact that they are not indicates that the war on poverty has not marched forward with a string of unambiguous victories.

More than five years after the passage of the Economic Opportunity Act the war on poverty has barely scratched the surface. Most poor people have had no contact with it, except perhaps to hear the promises of a better life to come. In terms of impact on the poor, it is quite clear, though discouraging, that "the most effective antipoverty program of the 1960's was the Vietnam war."[1] This is not quite accurate, since it was not the war but the public expenditures it engendered, with the consequent generation of incomes and tightening of the labor market. Public expenditures on nonmilitary purposes would have done as well or better, but it is obvious that the resources devoted to the war on poverty have not been sufficient to do the job.

In his recent book, which provides the most comprehensive

[1] Sar A. Levitan and Garth L. Mangum, "Programs and Priorities," *The Reporter* (Sept. 7, 1967), p. 22.

evaluation of the Office of Economic Opportunity and its programs published to date, Sar A. Levitan reaches just this conclusion, and concludes further, as the present author does, that OEO's major successes have been in its role as spokesman for the poor:

> As long as society continues grudgingly to provide help to the poor, as manifested by the poor laws over the centuries, we must settle for improving the administrative efficiency of the 1964 poor law and augmenting its operations. Therefore, the continuance in the federal Establishment of an agency whose sole mission is to help the poor and to help design new exits from poverty is appropriate. For the foreseeable future it appears that the biblical admonition that "the poor shall never cease out of the land" will hold for our society.[2]

As was pointed out in earlier chapters, expenditures on the poor have increased in recent years. These have been mostly in the health field, with Medicare and Medicaid; in education, primarily with the Elementary and Secondary Education Act of 1965; and in increased aid to the aged and to public assistance recipients, with the social security amendments of 1965 and 1967. Not all of the expenditures under this new legislation have gone to the poor, but a considerable amount has. New legislation thus far has done little for the housing situation, has made no start on a comprehensive income maintenance plan,[3] and has largely ignored the job creation problem except for minor amendments to the Economic Opportunity Act.

One thing that has become clear is that the poverty problem in central cities is more difficult than had been thought. Indeed, there is some evidence that poverty in some neighborhoods of some central cities is growing worse rather than better.[4] In particular, the problem of employment among the hard-core poor has turned out to be unyielding. We saw in Chapter 5 that even when employment was essentially what has come to be regarded as full, large numbers of the hard core cannot find jobs. Training these

---

[2] *The Great Society's Poor Law: A New Approach to Poverty* (Johns Hopkins Press, 1969), p. 318.

[3] If Congress adopts the recommendations in President Nixon's welfare message of 1969, a start will be made on comprehensive income maintenance.

[4] For example, a news story reported that a study by Fordham University financed by OEO indicated that poverty had worsened in the Bronx. *New York Times*, Sept. 3, 1967.

people is much more complicated than had been thought, involving attitudes, motivation, literacy, speech, and many other things that were not anticipated. All of this adds expense to the task, and time. The government has learned a great deal in the last few years about the poorest people in the labor market, and everything learned points to the difficulties of the job ahead.

As we look at what the government has tried to do in the war on poverty, it is worth stressing once more that the novel element in the picture has been the Office of Economic Opportunity. A panel of Americans studied the situation carefully and in March 1968 reported to the President and nation as follows: "The Office of Economic Opportunity in little more than 3 years has made significant progress. It spends less than 10 percent of the funds paid out by the Federal Government to help the poor, the aged, and the underprivileged, but its impact has been without precedent."[5]

One of the very real accomplishments of OEO, both at national and at local levels, is that it has become the spokesman for the poor. In councils of government, in cabinet meetings, and at the grass roots, there is now an organization to represent the poor, and this has had its impact, as can be seen in the attempts to eliminate the agency on the ground that it is wasteful and duplicative. In a sense it has been duplicative, or has threatened to be on occasion, and this is one way it has achieved some real institutional improvements. For example, until 1965 the only public Employment Service office in Chicago was located in the Loop, where the poor rarely go. Today Employment Service personnel are in every neighborhood service center in Chicago, having been goaded to this by the threat that if necessary a competing employment office would be set up by the community action agency. As another example, adult literacy classes under OEO have been taught by trade union officers and others who have no state education department certification. For a while it seemed as though this development might break the bottleneck of the adult teacher shortage.

Of all the OEO programs it is clear that the most interesting is community action. The National Advisory Council had this to

[5] National Advisory Council on Economic Opportunity, *Focus on Community Action* (1968), p. xi.

say: "What is particularly impressive and exciting is the new idea of community action programs. Stirring hope among the poor, they are bringing opportunity and offering responsibility to the disadvantaged. They are making possible participation and communication on the part of those who have been rejected, excluded, alienated, and neglected."[6] The council made it clear that it was the local-option part of CAP that they found particularly promising, and with this view the writer is in agreement. This is not because it can be said that money spent in this way is best; it is simply that the promise seems to lie in this direction and should be tested to the limit.

If this has validity, there are some developments that are to be deplored. One is the tendency to earmark CAP funds, begun by the agency and taken up by the Congress with enthusiasm. National emphasis programs may be very good, but they reduce the funds available for local option. In fiscal 1968 there was $338 million for local initiative CAP after Congress had completed earmarking, and $370 million in 1969. Spread over more than 1,000 community action agencies this is not much. The National Advisory Council believed that, although legislation now does not establish binding priorities on funds, "earmarking, de facto, is still in effect."[7]

A second development that will impinge adversely on local initiative is the question of local control. Until recently some 80 percent of the community action agencies had been private nonprofit agencies.[8] Most of them had made their peace with local governmental units and most had representation from local officialdom. In 1967 the Congress amended the statute to require that by July 1, 1968, all community action agencies be either political subdivisions, or agencies designated by a political subdivision. OEO's director was given bypass authority where an agency was not designated or did not perform satisfactorily. The impact of this amendment appears not to have been as substantial as originally expected and feared, though it could become important if activity on the community action front should accelerate in the future.

[6] *Ibid.*
[7] *Ibid.*, pp. 28, 52.
[8] *Ibid.*, p. 19.

Basic to all other problems is the lack of resources to do the job. All forms of public assistance are now reaching about 10 million of the poor, two out of five or 40 percent. Furthermore, in almost every case people receiving welfare are not brought out of poverty. It was stated in Chaper 5 that the experts estimated that for every ten persons in need of manpower training, existing programs are reaching one. It is not known how many people CAP is reaching but it can only be a small fraction. Of the 600 poorest counties in the United States (the poorest fifth), 215 are not served at all by a community action agency.[9]

It is crystal clear that the gap between requirements and expenditures is not being filled by OEO. Let us look briefly at the fiscal history of OEO. It was first funded in October 1964 at $800 million for fiscal 1965. Since spending hardly started before the first of the year, this funding in effect was for a half year. Furthermore, since the spending began at zero and built up over the months, if the $800 million were to be spent by the end of the fiscal year, the rate of spending in the latter part of the half year would have had to be substantially above $800 million for six months.

The President asked for $1.5 billion for fiscal 1966, which he referred to on more than one occasion as a "doubling" of the appropriation.[10] It was not, of course. There does not seem to be great subtlety in the notion that $1.5 billion for twelve months is about the same as $800 million for six. Indeed, because of the growing rate of spending by the new agency, the $1.5 billion appropriated by the Congress for 1966 actually caused cutbacks. For 1967 the President asked $1.75 billion; $1.6 billion was appropriated at first, and a supplemental appropriation added $75 million. The 1968 appropriation was $1.773 billion; for 1969 it was $1.948 billion; and for 1970 it was $2.048 billion.[11] It is thus generally accurate to say that there has been no increase in funds available since the program started, though it was clearly expected that appropriations would grow substantially beyond the initial funding level.

A good part of the explanation for this is the Vietnam war, or at

[9] *Ibid.*, p. 38.

[10] See, for example, *The Budget of the United States Government for the Fiscal Year Ending June 30, 1966*, p. 118.

[11] *Congressional Quarterly Weekly Report*, Oct. 17, 1969, p. 2002.

least this came to be the excuse. Decisions to escalate were made in the spring of 1965, and it became apparent that war costs were going to mount ominously. For this reason, nonwar expenditures were cut back or kept from expanding in order to accommodate the growing military budget. This was done by the executive; the legislative pressures at that time were for expanding the war on poverty. The nation was wealthy enough to afford it, and indeed President Johnson on several occasions said we could fight both wars at once. But the lid stayed firmly on.

One danger of a continuation of budgets of these sizes is that they tend to become institutionalized in people's minds. When appropriations have been between $1.5 and $2 billion for four or five years, there is an inclination to think of $2.5 billion as a substantial increase. The fact is that there is no real difference between $2 and $2.5 billion; neither will make an impact on the problem we confront. What is called for is a tripling, or more, not small increments, and as each year passes with budget levels remaining essentially constant, this becomes more difficult to achieve, and spokesmen for the program become more reluctant to press for significant changes—they fear they will not be taken seriously.

A logical question that stems from this is whether the war on poverty should have been started. Should it not be suspended now until the day when the Vietnam war ends, or resources become more plentiful for other reasons? The point is sometimes made that the program has raised expectations among the poor and has increased bitterness among them by failing to deliver. This is sometimes said to lie back of the riots that have come to characterize our summers of late. After the Detroit riots of July 1967, Mayor Jerome P. Cavanagh was quoted as follows: "What we've been doing, at the level we've been doing it, is almost worse than nothing at all. . . . We've raised expectations, but we haven't been able to deliver all we should have. . . ."[12]

The sociologists will have to tell us whether this theory of social development is valid or not. It is asserted, and it does sound plau-

[12] J. Anthony Lukas, " 'Whitey Hasn't Got the Message,' " *New York Times Magazine*, Aug. 27, 1967, Pt. 1, p. 58.

sible. But even if valid, the questions posed are not real ones. We are not going to call off the war on poverty, short of a drastic and improbable reversal of the nation's political direction. It became clear shortly after the Republican victory in the 1968 elections that the war on poverty will not end. The new administration's first domestic message assured its continuance. It has changed in form,[13] to be sure, and will change more, but one does not turn off a set of programs like these, with all their nationwide organization, and turn them on again a few years later. There is no spigot labeled "services for the poor" which can be turned on and off at will. The real question is whether the poverty apparatus can be held together until resources are made available to do the job acceptably.

The experience in the last few years has not revealed what is the ideal set of weapons for a genuine war on poverty. But we have been learning. There is better understanding of the training problems in urban and rural slums; it is evident that a massive effort will be required. Income maintenance efforts have been judged unsatisfactory. The participation of the poor has been found valuable, and there has been some success in getting that participation. We need a varied set of weapons, and we strongly suspect that community action has a central role to play.

Above all it is manifest that all this costs money. We are told that we must wait until the Vietnam war comes to an end. There is fervent hope that it will end soon, but if it does not, we may not be able to wait much longer to get on with the "other war." If Vietnam ends, the resources will be more readily available;[14] if it does not, the writer would argue that the resources are there anyway. Disposable income (that is, income after taxes) is over $600 billion and has been increasing at some $35 to $40 billion per year. To begin to make real progress in the elimination of poverty would require a small fraction of the increase each year. In other words, incomes would not be cut to make the effort; making

[13] See Chap. 4.

[14] It is becoming stylish now to deny this, on the ground that the military budget and other program commitments will devour most of the slack. This may indeed happen, but if it does, it will be the result of a conscious policy decision, and a bad one.

the effort would simply reduce somewhat the extent to which we are all richer each year than the previous year.

We have made the commitment, at least verbally. We have developed the tools and found that some of them work. We have the resources, even in the face of continued high military budgets, and without requiring sacrifices. We should get on with the job.

Index